The Screenplay Outline Workbook

NAOMI BEATY

A step-by-step guide to brainstorm ideas, structure your story, and prepare to write your best screenplay

COPYRIGHT AND PERMISSIONS

The Screenplay Outline Workbook: A step-by-step guide to brainstorm ideas, structure your story, and prepare to write your best screenplay

Copyright © 2022 by Naomi Beaty / writeandco.com. All rights reserved.

Copyright
No part of this publication may be reproduced, distributed, stored, or transmitted in any form or by any means, including photocopying, scanning, recording, or other electronic or mechanical methods, without the prior written permission of the author or publisher.

Limit of liability/disclaimer of warranty: While the author and publisher have made every effort to provide you with their best advice and strategies within this workbook, they make no guarantees, representations, or warranties with respect to the accuracy or completeness of the contents of this document. The content herein may not be suitable for your situation. Neither the publisher nor author shall be liable for any outcome.

Permissions
Feel free to photograph or film this planner for the purposes of review or social media sharing. Do not photograph and/or film the planner in its entirety.

Table of Contents

Introduction 9

    Who am I and why this workbook? 9
    But doesn't outlining suck the creativity out of writing? 10
    What's in this workbook? 11
    What can this workbook do for you? 12
    Download additional resources 13

Section 1: Choosing Your Screenplay Idea 17

    Three Idea-Generating Exercises 17
        Exercise #1: New Point of View 17
        Exercise #2: ROP + Fantasy 26
        Exercise #3: Headliners 30
    Choosing an Idea for Your Next Screenplay 36
        What kind of idea works best in a screenplay? 36
        Is my screenplay idea too simple? 37
        Can it be a movie or should it be something else? 37
        Is the journey, adventure, or mission difficult enough to support a movie? 38
        Other factors to consider 40
    You Have a Screenplay Idea! Now What? 42
        Brain dump prompts 42

Section 2: Building the Story Foundation With the 4 Essential Elements 49

    Who Wants What? 49
    Foundation Elements 49
    Whose Story Is It? 50
        What makes an effective protagonist? 50
        Protagonist examples 51
        Your screenplay's protagonist 52
    What Are They Trying to Achieve? 53
        What makes an effective story goal? 53
        Goal vs. method 54
        Goal examples 55
        Your screenplay's story goal 56
    What's Standing in the Way? 58
        What makes an effective opposing force? 58
        Antagonist examples 59
        Your screenplay's antagonist or main force of opposition 60
    Why Do They Want It? 62
        What makes effective stakes? 62
        Examples of stakes 63
        What's at stake in your screenplay 64

Celebrate! You have the essentials 65

Section 3: Finding the Shape of the Story With 3-Act Structure 75

The Central Dramatic Question 75
    Answering the CDQ 76
    CDQ examples 77
    What's your CDQ? 78
The Purpose of Each Act 79
    3-act examples 80
    Brainstorm what happens in each act of your screenplay 80

Section 4: Developing the Main Character 89

Transformation 89
    Transformation examples 90
    Transformation and Theme 90
    The "What I've learned..." exercise 91
    Matching character arc to plot 94
    Transformation brainstorm 94
Defining Characteristic 97
    Defining characteristic examples 97
    Defining characteristic brainstorm 98
The Protaganist's Introduction 102
    Getting us hooked on the protagonist 102
    Protagonist introduction brainstorm 104
    Introducing your protagonist 106
Have a character but no plot? 108

Section 5: Creating the Screenplay's Framework with Six Major Plot Points 115

What Are the Major Plot Points? 115
How to Know Where a Plot Event Should Go 116
Functions of the Major Plot Points 117
    Inciting Incident 117
    Break into Act 2 117
    Midpoint 118
    Low Point* 118
    Break into Act 3 119
    Climax* 119
Figuring Out Your Story's Major Plot Points 119
Major Plot Points Examples 120
Major Plot Points Brainstorm 121

Celebrate! You've built the foundation and framework for your story! 125

Section 6: Expanding the Cast of Characters to Work With the Main Character 129

How Do Supporting Characters Create Change? 129
Four Common Ways Supporting Characters Challenge Protagonists ... 129
    Challenge #1: A New Worldview 129

TABLE OF CONTENTS

 Challenge #2: Faith in Self..*130*
 Challenge #3: Cautionary Tale..*130*
 Challenge #4: Aspirational Model...*131*
Supporting Character Brainstorm..132

Section 7: Putting It All Together in the Screenplay Outline..................................**141**

What Is a Screenplay Outline?...**141**
 First, process...*142*
 Next, format..*142*
 What goes into an outline?..*143*
Simple Story Chart..**144**
 A basic story arc template...*144*
 Simple story chart example...*146*
 Your simple story chart:..*148*
Notecards..**150**
 What goes on each card?..*150*
 What's the difference between a plot point and a beat and a scene?..................*151*
 Tips for getting started with notecards...*151*
 Does the Break into Act 2 go at the end of Act 1 or the beginning of Act 2?......*152*
 Notecarding your story..*153*
Sequences and Springboards..**153**
 Why use sequences in your screenplay?...*153*
 How do Sequences & Springboards work?..*154*
 What goes in a sequence?...*155*
 Sequences & Springboards example...*155*
 Your Sequences & Springboards...*157*
 Sequence prompts..*157*
 Incorporating character arc, relationship arcs, subplots....................................*168*
Diagram your story..**172**
Your Screenplay Outline..**184**
Screenplay Outline Example – *A Quiet Place* **184**
 Sequences & Springboards...*185*
 Breaking down sequences into beat ideas..*186*
 Expanding the beat list..*188*
 Beat/scene list screenplay outline..*193*
 Full scene-by-scene outline excerpt...*196*

When to stop outlining and start writing your screenplay..................................**203**

How to Vet Your Screenplay Outline Before Writing Pages... 204
A 40-Point Checklist... 204

How Do You Know When You're Done Outlining a Screenplay?..........................**207**

A few final words..**209**

Introduction

Who am I and why this workbook?

But doesn't outlining suck the creativity out of writing?

What's in this workbook?

What can this workbook do for you?

Download additional resources

Introduction

Who am I and why this workbook?

Hello and welcome! I'm glad you're here.

I'm Naomi Beaty and in this workbook I'll show you how to craft a rock-solid screenplay outline. In order to do that, we'll cover everything you need to know to design your story from scratch.

This book is a reflection of years of experience working with stories from a bunch of different angles: development, producing, pitching, writing, and teaching. I hope it's the wise but gentle guide that will meet you where you are and lead you to your destination. The set of tools, exercises, and information you need to turn your ideas and inspiration into a functional outline that will help you write your best screenplay yet.

As a story consultant and screenwriting instructor with two decades of experience in the film and television industry, I've read thousands of scripts, advised hundreds of writers, and worked with screenwriters, producers, and directors at all career levels – from brand new to successfully established in the industry today. With the projects they've brought to me for consultation, my clients have placed in prestigious screenwriting contests, gained representation, pitched to every major studio, and have optioned or sold feature screenplays and TV pilots to producers.

I started in the industry as an assistant to producer/manager Craig Baumgarten, went on to work in development at Madonna and Guy Oseary's Maverick Films, and then alongside Blake Snyder analyzing fifty movies for his second book, *Save the Cat! Goes to the Movies* – a true crash course in movie structure! Later I taught the Save the Cat weekend intensives in Los Angeles.

After working 1-on-1 with writers and filmmakers for about a decade, I created the "Idea to Outline" and "Finish Your Screenplay" workshops so that I could help more writers by targeting the parts of the process where they most often asked for help: outlining a screenplay, and then finishing a first draft.

When writers come to me for guidance in either of these two areas, what they're really asking is, "*How do I get my ideas onto the page?*" They have a movie idea (or several) they're excited to write. But, for one reason or another, they're stuck.

Maybe they started writing but found themselves stranded thirty pages into the script without any idea how to move forward. Maybe they're unsure where to start at all, and the task of going from idea to finished screenplay feels too big and intimidating.

Maybe they've read a bunch of how-to books but still feel confused about the actual steps to take. Maybe they're experiencing a little fear and hesitation around wanting to do their story idea justice.

Maybe they've even written screenplays before, but it was such an arduous process that they're reluctant to jump in again without a better strategy for writing the next one.

The writers I work with often hear me say it's better to finish one screenplay than to start and not-finish ten. This is simply because you learn so much by experiencing each part and the process as a whole.

But what's the best way to finish a screenplay? Do you jump straight in and keep writing until the end?

Every writer must find their own best process. Diving in without thinking works for some writers. On the other hand, I've seen a lot of first drafts that were written (or half-written, let's be honest) with that "write first, think later" method. And very often, a draft written without some advance planning will end up being a bigger mess than the writer wants or knows how to approach in a rewrite.

So how do you write a complete, usable first draft? One thing that I've seen help so many writers – even those who didn't think of themselves as "plotters" – is a strong plan. A map of your story. In other words, an outline.

But doesn't outlining suck the creativity out of writing?

This book is inspired by the work I do with writers, both in workshops and in 1-on-1 consulting. Whether we're discussing the early stages of story development or how to revise a completed draft of their screenplay, the underlying aim of our work together usually comes down to figuring out what story they want to tell and then making sure they're building a screenplay that conveys that story, clearly and entertainingly.

Throughout the process, I ask a lot of questions and together we find the answers that the writer feels ring true. It's not about imposing one particular system or set of "rules." It's about finding *their* best story. Showcasing the story they want to tell. Giving them the perspective to see it clearly so that they know what to write.

Planning what you'll write before you sit down to write the screenplay itself doesn't mean you'll end up with something lifeless or formulaic. It simply means you're working with the creative spark in a different form – perhaps at a stage of the process you've been neglecting up to now. It also means by the time you do face the blank page, you're well prepared and confident in the story you're telling. Which frees you to get creative with characters and dialogue and discovering the kind of magical, cinematic moments that made us all fall in love with movies in the first place.

Doing this creative heavy lifting *before* you're staring at the blank page can make the whole idea of writing feel less daunting. Sometimes that space between deciding to write and actually doing it is where we get stuck. The magnitude of the task just seems too much.

But when you approach the work as a manageable set of steps to help you explore your ideas and discover what works, it's easier to set aside whatever fear you're dealing with and get yourself to take action. It doesn't feel like work. It doesn't even feel like *writing*. (Which is sometimes exactly what a writer needs.)

Before I became a teacher and consultant, I also worked as a screenwriter myself. I've been hired to write screenplays, both original and adapted from other source material. And I even have a project still currently under option.

All this to say, I have firsthand experience from the writer's side as well, and in this workbook I've tried to create the resource I wish I'd had each time I set out to write a screenplay. These are the steps I still use when I'm figuring out how a story works, whether for myself or alongside a student or client.

What's in this workbook?

Simply put, this workbook will give you a set of steps and exercises to make outlining your screenplay a manageable process.

But what does it mean to outline your screenplay? Ask a million writers and you may get a million different answers.

What we're really talking about is the pre-writing part of the process. Pre-writing is everything you do before sitting down to write the screenplay itself. It's the exploring, developing, figuring out, and planning of the screenplay you're going to write... including crafting an outline.

In this workbook, I've included information and exercises to help you through all of it. Enough instruction and theory so that you know what you need to know, but not so much that it overwhelms you before you even get started. Room to work through your story ideas and collect your notes and flashes of brilliance. An organized place to keep what you discover about your story as you develop it so that you can easily reference it when needed.

We'll cover the pre-writing process in 7 sections:

1. Choosing your screenplay idea
2. Building the story foundation with the four essential elements
3. Finding the shape of the story with 3-act structure
4. Developing the main character
5. Creating the story's framework with six Major Plot Points
6. Expanding the cast of characters to complement and challenge the main character
7. Putting it all together in the screenplay outline

Each section is further divided into individual lessons and action steps to help you focus and create the next piece of your story's big picture. This method is for you whether you're brand new to screenwriting and need help getting started, or you've written screenplays before but want to be more efficient at it.

If you've tried to write a screenplay before but found yourself stuck somewhere in Act 2, having an outline that serves as a map of your screenplay can make all the difference in getting you to that *Fade Out* finish line. And a well-planned first draft ultimately requires fewer drafts and less rewriting overall.

What can this workbook do for you?

This workbook is meant to be a hands-on experience. You can start with just a seed or inkling – or nothing at all, even! – and end up with a solid story premise, compelling characters, and an outline that provides a blueprint for writing your screenplay draft. Each section contains prompts to get you thinking about the aspects of your story that will be most helpful and important as you approach your screenplay.

But the final intention of this workbook is to give you a way to start and create momentum while you're feeling the spark of enthusiasm. Because sometimes starting is the hardest part.

It's easy to get in our heads and psych ourselves out about wanting to do it "right." So it can be helpful to take a step back and remember that starting is just one step in the process. The only way it's going to make or break you is if you don't do it.

I love this Arthur Ashe quote as a mindset reminder:

"Start where you are. Use what you have. Do what you can."

If you feel nervous about starting – lean on the workbook and take it one small step at a time. The workbook sections will guide you in creating the foundation for your screenplay, piece by piece. With each exercise, you'll explore ideas and make choices inspired by, and that give rise to, the story you want to tell. Along the way, you'll build your screenplay, even when it doesn't feel like outlining – or even writing – at the moment.

INTRODUCTION

After you've done the work of this workbook, you will have a well-planned outline for your screenplay. But more than that, you'll have a process you can use again and again, for each of your future screenplays. Take the steps and make them your own. Find what works best for you.

Use this workbook to explore, discover, and create. Keep moving forward. Tell us your story.

Download additional resources

Find PDF copies of worksheets, bonus content, and more at
https://writeandco.com/outline-workbook

SECTION 1

Choosing Your Screenplay Idea

Three Idea-Generating Exercises

Exercise #1: New Point of View

Exercise #2: ROP + Fantasy

Exercise #3: Headliners

Choosing an Idea for Your Next Screenplay

What kind of idea works best in a screenplay?

Is my screenplay idea too simple?

Can it be a movie or should it be something else?

Is the journey, adventure, or mission difficult enough to support a movie?

Other factors to consider

You Have a Screenplay Idea! Now What?

Brain dump prompts

Choosing Your Screenplay Idea

This section is all about igniting and capturing the spark of inspiration – the very first step in writing your screenplay.

Of course, a movie idea that you can't stop thinking about may be exactly what led you here. If you've already identified one story idea that you can't wait to turn into a screenplay, then great! You can skip this section.

But if that's not the case, and you don't have a single screenplay idea yet, there's no need to panic. This section contains three exercises you can use to come up with new story concepts anytime you need them. Try one, try them all. Generate a bunch of ideas, even if they feel half-baked right now. Later on in the process you'll figure out which ones have legs, and then narrow in on which one you might want to write first.

And if you're somewhere in the middle – maybe you already have a few contenders but don't know which to tackle right now, or maybe you're unsure whether you're excited enough about any of them to jump in – then it's your choice:

Try the exercises here and you just might find a new idea that jumps to the front of your writing queue.

Or, feel free to skip ahead to the "How To Choose An Idea" section for now. There, you'll find questions to help you evaluate the ideas you have and narrow in on the one you'll write. You can always come back here and hatch some new options whenever you want.

Three Idea-Generating Exercises

The three exercises here are meant to be fun, stress-free opportunities to let your imagination go wild. Like a good brainstorming session, no idea is a bad idea. Even if something you come up with doesn't quite hold up on its own, combine it with other ideas and tweak it a bit and you might have something great. Nothing has to be fully formed at this point, either. We're just generating sparks of inspiration. Enjoy the process!

Exercise #1: New Point of View

Step 1: Start with any existing legend, fairytale, or public domain property.

By way of example, I'll start with the story of Mulan, the legendary Chinese woman warrior who disguised herself as a man in order to join the army.

Step 2: Brainstorm different points of view on this story's events.

Think about and list the other characters who could know about or be involved in the story's events, or who might otherwise care about them in some way.

For my Mulan example, maybe I'd come up with:

- Mulan's sister or brother
- A fellow soldier
- A soldier from an enemy force
- Mulan's great-great-great-great granddaughter
- A royal from the Han Dynasty who recruits spies for special missions

Let your brain go where it wants, and write down as many ideas as you can capture.

Step 3: Identify what story ideas or types emerge naturally.

Each of these points of view suggests different story possibilities. With Mulan's sister, maybe we get a sibling rivalry. With a fellow soldier, maybe there's an epic forbidden romance. And so on. You might even come up with several possible stories for one POV.

Ultimately you might generate a fresh spin on a classic story that you're excited to write. (As the 2012 film *Snow White and the Huntsman* did for the familiar fairytale.)

Or you might come up with an interesting dynamic that inspires a new original story, rather than adapting the source material you started with.

For my example, maybe I'd decide I would rather write a story of female sibling rivalry set in the contemporary world of the U.S. Marine Corps. I got there by way of Mulan, using that story to spark ideas. But I've followed the details that interest me most and formed my own original idea, instead of writing the story of Mulan.

Remember, you're just generating new possibilities now. Later you'll choose which idea to develop more. But you're more likely to find a story you are passionate or curious or excited enough about to spend the next several months writing if you have many options to choose from.

Try exercise #1

There are blank charts below for brainstorming your ideas, and here's an example of how I might fill out the chart using Mulan as the starting point:

1: CHOOSING YOUR SCREENPLAY IDEA

The chosen source material: <u>Mulan – woman warrior who disguised herself as a man in order to join the army</u>

Point of View	Story Type or Idea	Notes
Mulan's sister or brother	A sibling rivalry	Two strong female leads could be interesting set in a military arena.
A fellow soldier	Forbidden love / romance	
A soldier from an enemy force	Suspenseful cat-and-mouse thriller	
Mulan's great-great-great-great granddaughter	Parallel stories in two different timelines	
A royal from the Han Dynasty	Twisty, actiony spy thriller	Maybe he's a recruiter for spies on special missions?

THE SCREENPLAY OUTLINE WORKBOOK

Your chosen source material: _____

Point of View	Story Type or Idea	Notes

Notes: _____

_____

_____

_____

1: CHOOSING YOUR SCREENPLAY IDEA

Your chosen source material: _____

Point of View	Story Type or Idea	Notes

Notes: _____
_____
_____
_____

THE SCREENPLAY OUTLINE WORKBOOK

Your chosen source material: _____

Point of View	Story Type or Idea	Notes

Notes: _____
_____
_____
_____

1: CHOOSING YOUR SCREENPLAY IDEA

Your chosen source material: _____

Point of View	Story Type or Idea	Notes

Notes: _____

_____

_____

_____

THE SCREENPLAY OUTLINE WORKBOOK

Your chosen source material: _____

Point of View	Story Type or Idea	Notes

Notes: _____
_____
_____
_____

1: CHOOSING YOUR SCREENPLAY IDEA

Your chosen source material: _____

Point of View	Story Type or Idea	Notes

Notes: _____
_____
_____

Exercise #2: ROP + Fantasy

Step 1: Take any life phase, rite of passage, or other universally understood situation, and add a fantasy (or supernatural, or sci-fi) element.

Step 2: Brainstorm "What if?" using both of those elements in as many different ways as you can.

For example, if I chose: "high school crush" for my universal experience and "ghosts" for my supernatural element, my brainstorm might come up with:

◇ What if a teenage girl died and came back to haunt the crush she never had the guts to approach when she was alive?
◇ What if a teen boy's high school crush died, and he started seeing her ghost everywhere, slowly driving him insane?
◇ What if a grown woman realized the ghost of her long-dead high school crush had been steering her life's direction for years?

Think about different character points of view you could make use of, and different ways the supernatural element could come into play. You can also try a variety of genres and tones for additional possibilities. After further development, maybe one of those ideas would have become the comedy *Over Her Dead Body*. Maybe it would have become the drama *Ghost*.

Try exercise #2

Life phase, rite of passage, or other universally understood situation:

_____

Fantasy, supernatural, or sci-fi element:

_____

What if...

_____

_____

1: CHOOSING YOUR SCREENPLAY IDEA

What if...
_____
_____

What if...
_____
_____

◆

Life phase, rite of passage, or other universally understood situation:
_____

Fantasy, supernatural, or sci-fi element:
_____

What if...
_____
_____

What if...
_____
_____

What if...
_____
_____

◆

Life phase, rite of passage, or other universally understood situation:
_____

Fantasy, supernatural, or sci-fi element:
_____

What if...

_____

_____

What if...

_____

_____

What if...

_____

_____

◆

Life phase, rite of passage, or other universally understood situation:
_____

Fantasy, supernatural, or sci-fi element:
_____

What if...

_____

_____

1: CHOOSING YOUR SCREENPLAY IDEA

What if...

_____

_____

What if...

_____

_____

◆

Life phase, rite of passage, or other universally understood situation:

_____

Fantasy, supernatural, or sci-fi element:

_____

What if...

_____

_____

What if...

_____

_____

What if...

_____

_____

◆

Exercise #3: Headliners

Step 1: Grab a newspaper, magazine, or tabloid headline that sounds interesting to you, and DO NOT read the story.

In this game, you'll take just the headline as your inspiration and twist it to come up with new stories.

Step 2: Use what you know about common movie types, tropes, and genres to pull out the different plots this headline suggests.

You can start by thinking of different story types and then ask, "How could this story be that type of movie?"

For example, a headline I saw today: "Garbage Collector Creates Library from Rescued Books." From this headline I could choose a few different story types and brainstorm ideas to fit those categories:

- How could this be a road trip movie?

When a garbage collector learns he only has six months left to live, he embarks on a cross-country road trip to locate the original owners of books that have personal inscriptions written in them.

- How could this be an inspirational underdog movie?

A garbage collector gathers discarded books and creates a free library for his struggling community, only to find himself in a David-and-Goliath struggle against the city library system.

- How could this be a conman movie?

A garbage collector uses his access and unique connections to steal back valuable first editions that were stolen from his father thirty years earlier – and which now reside in the private collection of the wealthiest man in America.

Here's a list of story types, genres, and tropes to prompt your brainstorming. This is certainly not an exhaustive list, so keep adding to it!

1: CHOOSING YOUR SCREENPLAY IDEA

Drama	Fantasy	Inspirational
Action	Horror	Rags-to-Riches
Adventure	Comedy	Comeuppance
Thriller	Thriller	Stalker
Romantic Comedy	Family	Body switch
Romance	Supernatural	Coming-of-age
Dramedy	Disaster	Wedding
Crime	Sports / Competition	Holiday
Western	Fairytale	Magical curse / powers
Musical	Forbidden love	Mentor
Sci-Fi	Fish-out-of-water	David-and-Goliath
Epic	Odd couple	Mistaken identity
Film noir	Heist	Monster attack
Period	Road trip	Rivalry
War	Monster in the house	Detective / mystery

Try exercise #3

There are blank charts below for brainstorming your ideas, and here's an example of how I might fill out the chart for the garbage collector story:

Headline: "Garbage Collector Creates Library from Rescued Books."

Story Type	New Concept
Road trip	*When a garbage collector learns he only has six months left to live, he embarks on a cross-country road trip to locate the original owners of books that have personal inscriptions written in them.*
Inspirational underdog story	*A garbage collector gathers discarded books and creates a free library for his struggling community, only to find himself in a David-and-Goliath struggle against the city library system.*
Conman	*A garbage collector uses his access and unique connections to steal back valuable first editions that were stolen from his father thirty years earlier – and now reside in the private collection of the wealthiest man in America.*

THE SCREENPLAY OUTLINE WORKBOOK

Headline: _____

Story Type	New Concept

Notes: _____

_____

_____

_____

_____

1: CHOOSING YOUR SCREENPLAY IDEA

Headline: _____

Story Type	New Concept

Notes: _____

_____

_____

_____

_____

THE SCREENPLAY OUTLINE WORKBOOK

Headline: _____

Story Type	New Concept

Notes: _____
_____
_____
_____
_____

1: CHOOSING YOUR SCREENPLAY IDEA

Headline: _____

Story Type	New Concept

Notes: _____

_____

_____

_____

_____

Now's your chance! If you haven't tried any of the story-generating ideas yet, give it a shot. Let your imagination go and see what you come up with.

Choosing an Idea for Your Next Screenplay

What if you have several movie ideas and you can't decide which one to work on first? For the eager or ambitious screenwriter, it might be tempting to outline multiple ideas at once.

But if you're at the beginning of your screenwriting learning curve or still figuring out your own best process, juggling ideas can end in frustration and overwhelm.

So, my advice? For now, choose one idea to work on. Take it all the way through the development, outlining, and writing process. You'll learn much more from finishing one project than from starting and not-finishing several.

And don't worry – you're not saying 'goodbye' to your other ideas! You're simply saying 'see you later.'

But how do you decide which idea to start with? Let's talk about the factors you may want to consider.

What kind of idea works best in a screenplay?

Keep it simple! Movies tend to be about one person's attempt to accomplish one thing and the transformative experience that is for them. Not always, but very, very often this is the case.

There are other characters involved in the story, of course. But look at something like *The Hunger Games* – it's Katniss's story. It's about her, the thing she's trying to do, how she's affected by it, and her emotional journey because of it, regardless of how many or how few other characters she interacts with.

Even if you don't realize it, some of your favorite movies are probably pretty simple stories at their core. A simple story has one main line of action or cause-and-effect pathway, such as:

> *Jaws* is about a guy trying to keep his town safe from a killer shark.
> *The Silence of the Lambs* is about a woman trying to stop a serial killer.
> *Notting Hill* is about a guy trying to date the pretty, popular girl.

All very simple in concept. It's the execution that makes them unique and memorable.

1: CHOOSING YOUR SCREENPLAY IDEA

Is my screenplay idea too simple?

Writers sometimes panic or feel disheartened that their simple story will result in a boring screenplay. (So if you're feeling this, you're not alone.)

There are a lot of things that can contribute to a movie that doesn't really grab us. Lack of meaningful stakes is a big one. Overly-familiar execution is another. (Don't worry – we'll talk more about these things soon.) But these aren't problems of a too-simple concept.

In fact, sometimes the stories that move us the most are very simple concepts that provide a showcase for genuine character drama and a powerful emotional experience for the audience.

A simple concept just gives you a clear framework and platform to demonstrate what's uniquely entertaining about your idea.

If you're writing one of your first screenplays, you will make your job easier and have a better learning experience if you practice on this type of story. So choose a simple idea – one that's centered on one clear protagonist who engages in one main conflict or line of action. Think "one person trying to achieve one thing."

If you can sum up your story idea to that effect, you likely have a perfectly simple story for your screenplay.

Can it be a movie or should it be something else?

For each of the ideas you're considering, think about whether it's really a movie or if it might be better suited for another medium. If you want to write a movie, you want to start with an idea that's meant to be a movie. If any of your potential projects make more sense as a TV series, a novel, a graphic novel, or something else, set those aside for now.

In general, a story that's well suited for a movie will be:

- ⋄ Closed ended (there will be some kind of resolution by the end of the movie).
- ⋄ Primarily about "one person trying to achieve one thing", or at least have one main conflict or cause-and-effect pathway.
- ⋄ Rooted in concrete, external actions that we can see play out on screen.

If your story is more internal (inside a character's head), it might be better suited as a novel. If it's about an ensemble of characters who each have their own stories going on, or if it's more open-ended, or so epic or wide-ranging that it would be difficult to limit it to one main line of action, it may be better suited to a TV series.

Is the journey, adventure, or mission difficult enough to support a movie?

The idea you choose has to sustain a whole movie. So whatever the main character is attempting to do or pursue shouldn't be too easy to achieve. (Or you may have a very short screenplay.)

Difficulty can come from one or more of these areas:

- The goal itself is so hard to achieve.
- The opposition is so strong.
- The stakes are so high.

We'll talk more about these areas in a later section, but for now think about each of your potential ideas through this lens. Does the objective or resolution seem hard enough that it can't be achieved too quickly? Does it seem likely that we can watch an entire movie about the character trying to do this one thing?

Screenplay Idea Scorecard

Use this chart to collect and compare the ideas you're considering. For each idea, ask:

- Does the story have a clear end point where we'll know whether the character has achieved their goal, solved their problem, or completed their mission?
- Are there obvious external actions we can see the character take as they attempt to achieve their goal?
- Does the goal, task, or mission seem difficult enough that we could watch a whole movie about it?

You can also jot down any notes and ideas you come up with as you're thinking through the categories. Those details and ideas may come in handy later on.

1: CHOOSING YOUR SCREENPLAY IDEA

Idea or Working Title	Clear end point?	External actions?	Enough to sustain a movie?
Example: *Erin Brockovich*	*Yes – if Erin can get PG&E to pay the people they've injured, then she's won.*	*She has to investigate to figure out how the people are being injured and who is responsible, then get the victims to agree to a class action suit, then carry out the legal action.*	*Yes! Erin is outmatched in legal knowledge and resources the whole way and the process has enough steps to sustain the movie.*

Other factors to consider

By now you've thought about which of your ideas is going to work best in screenplay form, but perhaps you still have a few options to choose from. If that's the case, here are other factors to consider when deciding what to write next:

Your purpose

What do you want this script to do for you?

Think about your goals as a writer. Are you just starting out, trying to write your first screenplay? Then choosing a more straightforward idea that sets you up for success* may be top priority.

(*Success being finishing the script, since you learn more by finishing one script than starting and not-finishing ten!)

Or maybe you've honed your craft and your voice, and now you want to write a breakout script that will get you noticed by producers or agents and managers. You'll probably want to think carefully about the concept, and make sure it's catchy enough to grab the industry's attention.

Or maybe you're already established but shifting the direction of your career. Do you want to write something that speaks to your new "brand" as a writer? Prioritize those projects that will represent you and help you transition into your next phase.

Figure out what you want your next writing project to do for you, and then weigh your list of projects against that goal. Some will fit the purpose more than others.

Your passion

Writing a screenplay is more of a marathon than a sprint but passion can carry you far. So weigh your enthusiasm for each project. Which ones make you excited to dive in?

Maybe you have an emotional connection with one of your projects that sets it apart from everything else. Maybe one of them is such a vivid concept that you've already thought of a million jokes or scenes, and you can't wait to get them onto the page. Maybe one is a personal story, based on a real event in your life that you want to share with the world, or that explores an issue you feel strongly about.

Whatever it is, think about which idea captures your attention and enthusiasm more than any other. If you could only write one (or one more) screenplay – ever – which would it be?

1: CHOOSING YOUR SCREENPLAY IDEA

You know the end

If everything else is equal and you still can't decide, my own personal advice is to go with the screenplay idea that you have a solid notion of how it ends.

Knowing the end means you know where you're headed. It gives you a destination to write toward. When you know the ending you can reverse-engineer setups and better figure out what needs to happen in the beginning and middle of the screenplay.

So if all else fails, choose the idea that you can see the ending to.

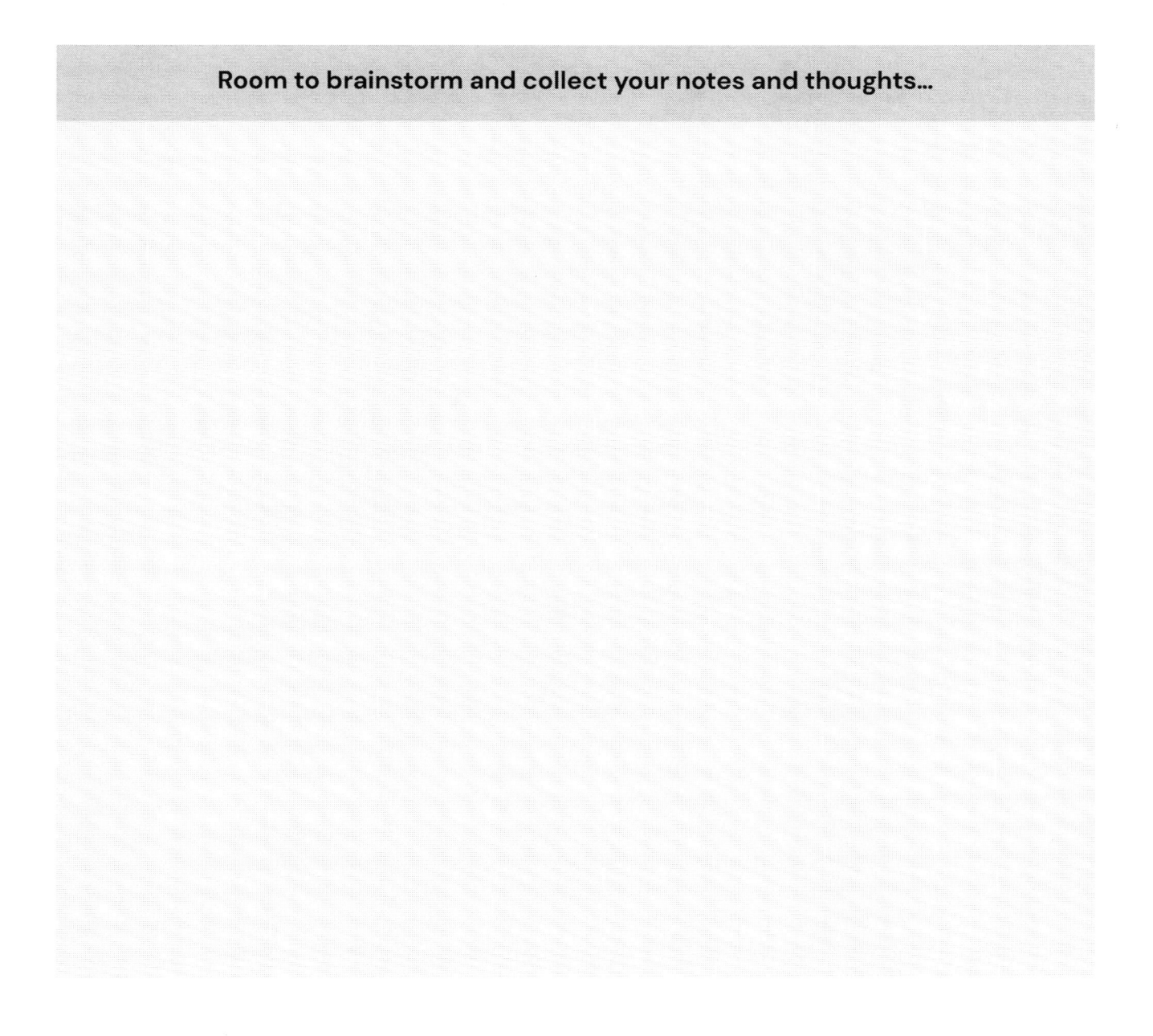

Room to brainstorm and collect your notes and thoughts...

You Have a Screenplay Idea! Now What?

First: celebrate! If you've decided which screenplay you're going to write, then you're on your way. First milestone passed.

And now let's ease into the process of developing and fleshing out your idea with one of my favorite exercises: the brain dump.

Really this is so easy it can hardly be called an exercise. How does it work? Simply free-write everything you know about your story idea, everything that makes you excited about it, everything you hope for it to end up being.

Anything at all that comes to mind when you think of your story or the movie it will become. Dump it all into one document. It's exciting to let your imagination go and just type (or hand-write) with abandon.

This exercise is a great way to capture some of the early enthusiasm you have for your project. Later on, if you're ever feeling adrift or unsure about your story, you can come back to this document and reconnect with what inspired you in the first place.

This exercise is also a way to collect all the random thoughts and details in your head into once place for safekeeping, so whatever form it takes is totally fine. You can make bullet-point lists, a mind map, a stream-of-consciousness ramble. Whatever feels easiest and most fun to you.

Since there's no other purpose for this document, there's no pressure to make it "good." The best version of a brain dump is the one that contains as much about your idea as you can think of.

Brain dump prompts

You can include in your brain dump anything that comes to mind about your project. And really, that's the way I'd encourage you to approach it: simply start writing, and put down anything and everything you know about this movie idea, however tentative or half-formed at the moment.

If that feels too broad or intimidating, here are a few prompts to help you get started:

- Write about the characters – who is involved in the story?
- What's important to these characters?
- How do the characters interact with each other? Describe their relationships or how they know each other.
- List or write about the things you think will happen in the movie, big or small.
- Describe any images that come to mind when you think about this story, even if

1: CHOOSING YOUR SCREENPLAY IDEA

you don't yet know what they mean.
- ◇ What excites you about this project?
- ◇ How did the idea originate? What inspired you?
- ◇ What will the finished movie look like or feel like?
- ◇ What does the soundtrack sound or feel like?
- ◇ Describe anything you'd love to see become part of the movie. Music, actors, locations, filmmakers you'd love to work with, etc.
- ◇ What other movies is it similar to?
- ◇ What's entertaining about this idea?
- ◇ What is the story about at its core?
- ◇ What values or questions does the story explore?
- ◇ How is the experience a defining or meaningful experience for the characters?
- ◇ What about the story makes it interesting or meaningful to you?

You may feel like you know very little so far and that's perfectly okay. Or you might write a lot but feel like what you've put down is chaotic or contradictory – that's okay too. You don't have to make any other decisions just yet. You're just collecting possibilities and sparks of inspiration, and memorializing what you love about your screenplay idea right now.

Room to brainstorm and collect your notes and thoughts...

Room to brainstorm and collect your notes and thoughts...

1: CHOOSING YOUR SCREENPLAY IDEA

Room to brainstorm and collect your notes and thoughts...

SECTION 2

Building the Story Foundation With the 4 Essential Elements

Who Wants What

Foundation Elements

Whose Story Is It?

What makes an effective protagonist?

Protagonist examples

Your screenplay's protagonist

What Are They Trying to Achieve?

What makes an effective story goal?

Goal vs. method

Goal examples

Your screenplay's story goal

What's Standing in the Way?

What makes an effective opposing force?

Antagonist examples

Your screenplay's antagonist or main force of opposition

Why Do They Want It?

What makes effective stakes?

Examples of stakes

What's at stake in your screenplay

Building the Story Foundation With the 4 Essential Elements

....

Shaping your story and ultimately crafting the screenplay isn't a linear process, but in general we'll move from macro to micro. We'll start by identifying the building blocks of the story, figuring out the plot and characters in broad strokes, and then we'll get progressively more and more granular.

But first, let's talk about what a story is so you have a big picture view of the landscape.

Who Wants What?

The majority of stories we see in movies – especially mainstream American movies – basically come down to "someone wants something badly and goes after it against strong opposition."

And you can see in that sentence the main components that a story needs: A someone. Something for them to go after. A reason they want it badly. And a source of conflict, something making the whole endeavor a challenge.

Right now, your spark of an idea may have all of these elements, just one, or anywhere in between. And wherever you're starting from is totally fine. In this section we're going to identify what you have and fill in the gaps so the foundation of your story is strong.

Foundation Elements

To put it in terms we'll use from here on, the foundation of the story is made up of:

- ◇ A protagonist (the someone).
- ◇ A goal (the something they want).
- ◇ An antagonist or main force of opposition (what's stopping them).
- ◇ Stakes (why they want it so badly).
- ◇ And a method or type of action they're taking to achieve the goal (what they're doing when they "go after" the thing they want).

If this feels confusing or too technical right now, don't worry – the next few sections will go into each of these elements, help you figure out the foundation elements of your story, and give you tips for making sure the elements are sturdy and the foundation is strong enough to build your story on. Let's take it one building block at a time.

Whose Story Is It?

I use the terms "protagonist," "main character," and "hero" all pretty interchangeably. We're talking about the one whose story it is.

The vast majority of movies are about one particular person pursuing one particular goal or trying to accomplish one particular thing.

When you think about your movie idea or your screenplay and how you might describe it to someone, you probably come up with some version of, "It's about this person who does this amazing/crazy/impossible thing…" Well, 9 times out of 10, your protagonist is the person you're describing with that simple pitch – the one doing the main thing the movie is about. Not always, but it's a good place to start when you're trying to figure out who your protagonist is.

But when it's not clear who that is, there are a few qualities we can look for in order to identify the protagonist.

According to Grammarly: "The most common definition of protagonist is the leading character of a drama or literary work." But what does it mean to be the "leading character"?

- ◇ We could think of it as the one in the spotlight. Our main focus in the story.
- ◇ We might also think of it as the one who "leads" the story by driving the plot forward with their actions and desires.

So let's start there: the protagonist is the character the audience is most focused on. If we're focused on them, that means they're compelling enough to capture our attention and interest. And if we're that interested, often it means we also empathize with them and root for them because we understand what they want and what's at stake.

As to the second point, the protagonist pushes the plot forward. That means they're doing something, trying to achieve something. They're taking action in pursuit of a goal or objective. Their actions drive the plot toward a resolution.

What makes an effective protagonist?

Remember, the protagonist is the one who is doing the thing the movie is about. So most importantly, you want a protagonist who has the ability to make choices and take actions that will drive the outcome. The protagonist should be active in the story.

2. BUILDING THE STORY FOUNDATION

If your protagonist can't or won't take action then they won't drive the story forward. Without someone doing that, the story will limp along or stall out altogether. And if the protagonist takes no action, your readers will likely get bored watching them.

Beyond that, you can also identify the best protagonist for your story by considering:

- Which character is likely to engage the audience's interest, curiosity, fondness, empathy, or admiration?
- Which character has the most to lose if they fail?
- Which character needs this journey the most?

The last question speaks to what a character can learn from going through the events we'll see in this movie. This is important because most movies are about transformation of some kind. (More on that in the transformation section). For now, simply thinking about which character might have the most to learn from this experience will put you on the right track.

Protagonist examples

In *Die Hard*, it's John McClane, a macho New York cop.
In *The Silence of the Lambs*, it's Clarice Starling, an ambitious FBI trainee.
In *The Ring*, it's Rachel, a journalist and single mom.
In *Bridesmaids*, it's Annie, a young woman who's stuck in a life rut.

In each of these examples, the protagonist character drives the action of the movie by *doing*. They are actively and urgently trying to solve problems or achieve goals. Each of them has a lot to lose should they fail and a lot to learn from what they're experiencing in the story.

What if you're writing an ensemble piece or a two-hander, like a romcom or a buddy comedy? You have a few options:

- You could think of the ensemble or group itself as the "main character" – like "a troop of fledgling Boy Scouts" or "a group of high school classmates assigned to Saturday morning detention" – and try to give each of them somewhat equal weight and attention in the screenplay.

- You could choose one central or point of view character to focus on and tell the story through his or her perspective, effectively making this character the protagonist as you develop your story.

- In the case of a romcom, buddy comedy, or other two-hander where there are two main characters who share a goal, you could think of them as co-protagonists, or you could choose one of the characters as the "primary" protagonist, knowing that the "secondary" character will get nearly equal weight.

- ⋄ Or – depending on the story and what each character is trying to accomplish – you might even find that one of the characters is the story's protagonist and one is the antagonist.

Your screenplay's protagonist

You might have known from the very beginning which character would be the protagonist of your story. If that's the case – great! Move on to the next section.

If you're having trouble figuring out or deciding who the protagonist should be in your screenplay, try thinking about these questions with your screenplay idea and its characters in mind.

- ⋄ Who is the focus of the story?
- ⋄ Which character has a clear goal or objective they're trying to achieve?
- ⋄ Who are we most likely to root for?
- ⋄ Which character can and will make decisions and take action to effect the outcome of the story?
- ⋄ Which character is likely to engage the audience's interest, curiosity, fondness, empathy, or admiration?
- ⋄ Which character has the most to lose if they fail?
- ⋄ Which character most needs the lesson or transformation this journey will provide?

Room to brainstorm and collect your notes and thoughts...

What Are They Trying to Achieve?

There's one thing at the heart of a movie's plot, and that is the story goal. The "story goal" is what the protagonist is trying to achieve by the end of the movie. It's what the entire story is structured around.

Watching the character attempt to achieve this thing – whatever that goal is – that *is* the movie.

The protagonist's goal is typically: established in the screenplay's setup (Act 1), pursued throughout the middle (Act 2), and achieved (or not) in the story's climax and resolution (Act 3). (More on this in the structure section.)

Identifying the story goal early in the process makes the job of plotting your story and writing it through to completion easier, because you have an engine to rely on – the pursuit of that goal.

A screenplay built around a clear goal is also generally more accessible to the reader. The pursuit of the story goal is an engine that carries us, the readers, through the narrative. Specifically, knowing the status of the goal (if it's been established, if it's being pursued, what conflicts are slowing the progress) orients us and makes us feel like this engine is reliable; we can relax and just enjoy the ride. If we're unsure what's going on with the goal — like if it isn't made clear when we expect it to be – we start to panic: "Am I lost? Where am I going? Why am I on this ride?"

The pursuit of the story goal is what moves the plot, and it's what the audience is tracking throughout the movie. When the audience knows the outcome of the goal the story is essentially over (although there is usually some wrapping up or showing us the effects of the outcome before the credits roll).

What makes an effective story goal?

There are as many possible story goals as there are movies, but some are easier to work with (and create a movie around) than others.

The story goal can be a concrete, external goal – like "to free the hostages" in *Die Hard*, or something more abstract or intangible – like "to open up about her trauma" in *Short Term 12*. But as you might guess, in the visual medium of movies, the more abstract or intangible the goal, the more you'll need to think about how to dramatize and externalize the action.

Here are a few additional things to consider when designing an effective story goal:

⋄ Degree of difficulty. A screenplay needs a goal that will take most of the movie to achieve. That means it should be difficult, either due to the nature of the goal itself, or because the opposition to the goal is so strong.

⋄ It's a process. Related to degree of difficulty, but a consideration of its own: be careful of story goals described as transitory actions. Meaning, if a character's goal is something that can be completed in one moment or one scene — such as to decide, or choose, or realize — you might not have enough story action to sustain a whole screenplay.

⋄ A visual indicator of success. Movie goals work best if there's a visual barometer for them — a defining image that captures victory. If the goal is something internal — like "to open up about her trauma" as in *Short Term 12* — it'll make your job as a writer easier if you can think of an external way to measure it.

Goal vs. method

There's one more thing that sometimes makes getting a handle on your story easier, and that's thinking about the action, method, or plan the protagonist is going to use to pursue the goal.

Defining the goal and the method separately can help you get clear on what the movie actually is. Not just in the big picture, but a sense of what we'll be watching on screen from scene to scene. Sometimes just identifying the story goal isn't quite enough to get that across and we need to identify the "method" element in order to grasp the experience and entertainment appeal of the movie. In a lot of cases, the "method" element is one of the main entertainment hooks of the screenplay — what makes it unique and distinct from other, similar movies.

For example, in the movie *The Silence of the Lambs*, Clarice's goal is to stop the serial killer Buffalo Bill. But the method she uses — and where much of the movie's entertainment comes from — is her interaction with Hannibal Lecter. So "befriending a notorious incarcerated psychopath" is the method Clarice uses to pursue her goal, and identifying that now will be a big help as you figure out and plan what happens in the screenplay.

Another example is the movie *Hell or High Water*. Protagonist Toby's goal is to deliver $40,000 to the bank by Friday in order to protect what's at stake, the family farm. But the method he's going to use is "robbing small-town branches of a local bank chain." That's what we're watching, and what's entertaining us throughout the movie.

So keep that in mind — it can make each of your decisions going forward much easier to navigate when you get a grasp on the difference between goal and method.

2. BUILDING THE STORY FOUNDATION

Goal examples

> In *Die Hard*, it's "save the hostages."
> In *The Silence of the Lambs*, it's "stop the serial killer."
> In *The Ring*, it's "stop the curse."
> In *Bridesmaids*, it's "to stop rival Helen from taking over as best friend and Maid of Honor."

Screenwriting guru Michael Hauge says that almost all movie goals fall into one of four categories: To Win, To Stop, To Escape, or To Retrieve. I'd add one more: To Deliver.

If you're having trouble defining your protagonist's goal, identifying which of those five general categories it falls into can help you tighten up your thinking. Also, if you know the general category you can brainstorm options and narrow in on the specific goal to build your screenplay around. And if you've identified the goal specifically for your story, but you feel that there's still something missing from the essence of the movie, think about whether there's a particular method the protagonist must engage in.

Some examples from produced movies:

To Win:

> General: To win (love).
> Specific: To win back his ex-wife. (*Silver Linings Playbook*)
> *Method: With the help of a young widow in the neighborhood, who he must help prepare for a dance competition.*

To Stop:

> General: To stop (a serial killer).
> Specific: Catch Buffalo Bill. (*The Silence of the Lambs*)
> *Method: By working with a notorious incarcerated psychopath.*

To Escape:

> General: To escape (the past).
> Specific: Return to his own time (the future). (*Back to the Future*)
> *Method: By enlisting the younger version of the time machine's inventor to help, while simultaneously attempting to make sure his parents meet and fall in love as they're intended, so as to have a future to return to.*

To Retrieve:

> General: To retrieve (money).
> Specific: Pull off a heist of a Las Vegas casino. (*Ocean's 11*)

Method: Through an intricately orchestrated heist involving eleven conmen, each with their own criminal specialty.

To Deliver:

General: To deliver (a bounty).
Specific: Return a bail-jumping mafia accountant to Los Angeles to stand trial. (*Midnight Run*)
Method: Traveling cross-country via train, car, and foot while attempting to stay one step ahead of the FBI, mafia henchmen, and a rival bounty hunter.

Your screenplay's story goal

To make sure the story goal is solid enough to build your screenplay around, see how it stacks up against the following criteria. If you find gaps or weak spots, think about what adjustments could strengthen the story goal.

- What is the protagonist trying to achieve by the end of the movie?
- If the goal is hard to define right now, can you firm it up using the five general categories?
- If you've identified a general category, is there a more specific description of the goal that will help crystallize what happens in your movie?
- Does the story goal tell us what we're watching in the movie, or do you need to identify the method the protagonist uses to pursue the goal in order to "see" the movie?
- Is the story goal difficult to accomplish?
- If you've identified a method, is it difficult to engage in?
- Does achieving the goal involve a process or a series of steps requiring more than one moment or scene?
- How will we know when the goal is achieved? (What is the visual indicator of success?)

2. BUILDING THE STORY FOUNDATION

Room to brainstorm and collect your notes and thoughts...

What's Standing in the Way?

"Where is the conflict coming from?" is one of the most important questions you can ask when planning and writing your screenplay.

Without conflict, there is no story. When the protagonist achieves his or her goal, the story is over – so if there's nothing significant standing in the way then it'll be a pretty short story.

Conflict in a screenplay can occur on many levels but here – as we're identifying the foundational pieces – we want to think about the main source of conflict, at the story level.

All movies have multiple conflicts, but the main conflict is the basis of the story. It's the thing the entire screenplay is built on, and creates the throughline or spine that everything else hangs off of. When you describe your story as "someone wants something and goes after it against strong opposition," you're describing the main conflict.

Earlier we covered the protagonist and the story goal. That's the "someone wants something" part of the equation. But conflict is created by opposing forces. Just as the protagonist pursues a goal, so does the antagonist. The antagonist's pursuit of a conflicting goal gives us the rest of the equation, the "...against strong opposition" part.

So let's put that next building block in place by figuring out who the antagonist is and what they want to achieve.

Note: The main force of opposition often shows up as an antagonist character, but it doesn't have to. For simplicity, I'll use the term antagonist here but just know –whatever form it takes, we're simply talking about the primary force of opposition that is (usually deliberately) getting in the way of your protagonist achieving the story goal.

What makes an effective opposing force?

Antagonists are not necessarily evil or villainous, though they can be. Antagonists also don't have to be human, or even sentient (consider *The Ring* or *Jaws* or *The Perfect Storm*).

What's most important in designing the antagonist is that they provide ample conflict for the protagonist. The antagonist should have a conflicting goal, that's key. It's also important that the antagonist be actively and consistently pursuing that goal (providing constant conflict). And very often the antagonist is at least as motivated as the protagonist is because he has something of his own at stake. If the antagonist is unmotivated or inactive, they won't provide enough conflict to keep the story going. The protagonist will achieve their story goal quickly, and the movie will be over.

But unlike the protagonist, the antagonist's goal isn't on a standardized timeline. That's because the movie is the protagonist's story. The protagonist's goal creates the timeline of the movie. Their goal is established in Act 1, pursued in Act 2, and resolved in Act 3. That's the basic framework for a screenplay.

The antagonist's goal, on the other hand, can exist before the start of the movie, be a reaction to learning of the protagonist's presence or goal, or it might line up with the protagonist's timeline. It depends on the story, and is informed by the nature of the opposing forces' interaction.

Not all main conflicts are constructed alike. But understanding this aspect of your story can help you figure out where, when, and how to introduce your antagonist and establish who wants what, when.

Antagonist examples

There are (at least) four different ways that opposing forces can interact to create conflict:

#1 The protagonist's goal can be to prevent the antagonist from achieving his goal.

For example, in *Bridesmaids*, protagonist Annie is Lillian's best friend and maid of honor. Antagonist Helen wants to take over both of those positions. Once Annie is aware of this, it's her goal to defend her position and stop Helen from taking over.

Another example is *The Silence of the Lambs*. Protagonist Clarice Starling wants to catch antagonist Buffalo Bill in order to stop him from killing women.

The Ring and *My Best Friend's Wedding* also land in this category.

#2 The antagonist's goal can be to prevent the protagonist from achieving his goal.

For example, in *The Babysitter*, protagonist Cole wants to see what his babysitter (the antagonist) is up to, then to escape once he learns she and her friends are killers who perform satanic rituals. The babysitter wants to stop Cole at every step.

#3 The protagonist and antagonist can both want the same goal, but only one can have it.

The movie *Warrior* falls into this category: estranged brothers both want to win the one MMA title that's up for grabs. Only one character can succeed. (Even though neither of them *feels* like a bad guy or villain, function-wise they represent the primary force of opposition for each other and so they are essentially each others' antagonist.)

#4 The antagonist's goal can be something separate from, but in conflict with, the protagonist's goal.

For example, in *Die Hard* the protagonist John McClane wants to save the hostages from the terrorists. Meanwhile, antagonist and head terrorist Hans Gruber wants to rob the vault in the Nakatomi building, and he's taken the hostages as part of his plan to do so.

If John McClane saves the hostages, Hans's plan to rob the vault will fail. If Hans succeeds, all of the hostages will die as part of his master plan. The pursuit of their goals makes the protagonist and antagonist the primary force of opposition for each other, even if their goals don't look mutually exclusive on their face.

Additional examples include *Finding Dory*, *The Perfect Storm*, and stories with similarly environmental or other non-sentient antagonists that are in the way of the protagonist trying to achieve their goal. The "antagonists" in these stories are just being or doing their natural thing, not necessarily trying to deliberately prevent what the protagonist wants to achieve. Yet the antagonists' existence presents the main force of opposition in the protagonist's pursuit of his goal.

Your screenplay's antagonist or main force of opposition

What's the main conflict in your story? If it's easier, think about what the protagonist's goal is, and then identify who or what is the main thing that's stopping them from achieving it.

If you're still unsure about the story's antagonist, think about the protagonist's goal, and then brainstorm other goals that would be in opposition. You can use the four types of main conflict as a starting point:

- ⋄ Who might want to stop the protagonist from achieving their goal altogether?
- ⋄ Or, conversely, who might be trying to achieve something that the protagonist needs or wants to stop?
- ⋄ Who might want to achieve the same goal as the protagonist, thereby getting in the protagonist's way?
- ⋄ What other goals would put another character in your protagonist's way?
- ⋄ Or are there any non-character forces that could serve as the main opposition to the protagonist's goal?

2. BUILDING THE STORY FOUNDATION

Room to brainstorm and collect your notes and thoughts...

Why Do They Want It?

There's one more thing to think about before we move on to plotting, and that's what is at stake in the story.

Stakes are, in a nutshell, whatever the main character stands to gain or lose, pending the outcome of the story. That's what's hanging in the balance, the negative consequences if the protagonist fails to achieve the goal. As in, the protagonist's life is at stake, or the safety of their child is at stake, or the character's family farm is at stake should they fail to get the money to the bank on time.

Stakes tell us what's important to the character, since whatever is at stake is what's motivating the character to take on the big, audacious thing they're doing in the story.

And stakes are a big factor in making the reader or audience care enough about the story to stay with you to the end. It's tough to stay engaged with a story if we don't understand why someone is pursuing their goal or if we're not emotionally invested in their pursuit.

Yes, a likeable or interesting character can initially hook the audience. But we need a reason to care about the story. That's what keeps us watching (or turning pages) – because when we care, when we're invested, we feel compelled to see the outcome.

The stakes will be raised throughout your story, and new stakes will come into play. But right now, as we're creating the sturdy foundation of your story, think about what's initially at stake: the primary thing that the protagonist is trying to protect by pursuing the story goal.

What makes effective stakes?

The stakes of a good story include both the concrete, external stakes and the intangible, internal stakes.

External stakes are usually a bit easier to grasp and to implement, so we'll focus there first. It's whatever concrete, external outcome will result if the protagonist fails to achieve the goal.

The most commonly used types of external stakes tend to be:

⋄ Safety or fate of a group (as in *Die Hard*, *Speed*, and *Gladiator*).

⋄ The life of either the protagonist or someone very important to them (as in *Die Hard*, *The Ring*, *The Silence of the Lambs*, *Taken*).

2. BUILDING THE STORY FOUNDATION

As you might have noticed, more than one type of stakes can be in play in a story, even initially.

And there are many, many types of stakes possible, beyond the two listed above. What's at stake in a story might be a person's livelihood (or financial survival, like in *Hell or High Water*), freedom (physical, mental, etc. like in *Get Out*), reputation, happiness, sanity, or access to something or someone very important or meaningful to them (like in *Bridesmaids*, or *Gifted*).

It's also useful to think about not only WHAT will happen (how the stakes will play out externally), but also WHY these stakes matter, or why we should care. These are the internal or emotional stakes.

Most simply, internal stakes are what the external stakes mean to the protagonist. What it all represents on a value-based, emotional, or even philosophical level. It's the 'why' that gives the external stakes emotional impact.

When the internal stakes have been established, the reader knows what emotional or internal impact the outcome of the story will have on the protagonist.

Examples of stakes

In the Pixar movie *Soul*, protagonist Joe wants to reunite his soul with his body. That's the story goal.

The external stakes? Joe's life. If he fails to reunite his soul with his body, he will pass on to the Great Beyond and no longer live on Earth. This is the concrete, external, or physical consequence of failing to achieve his story goal.

The internal stakes? If Joe fails to reunite his soul with his body, he will forever lose his chance to become a successful musician, to fulfill his passion and what he believes is his purpose in life. In short, his entire life will have been meaningless. That's what the external stakes mean to Joe, and what gives the story emotional impact.

What's at stake in your screenplay

Try walking your story through these questions to get clear on the external and internal stakes. (Refer to the *Soul* example above for guidance and inspiration.)

What is the protagonist's story goal?

_____
_____

What concrete, external consequence will occur if the protagonist fails at that goal?

_____
_____
_____
_____
_____

What would it mean to the protagonist if that external consequence occurs? What does that external consequence represent to the protagonist? What emotional experience would the protagonist endure? Or even more simply, WHY does the protagonist care so much about preventing the external consequence?

_____
_____
_____
_____
_____

2. BUILDING THE STORY FOUNDATION

Celebrate! You have the essentials

If you've worked through the previous sections and exercises, you now have a sturdy foundation for your story and your screenplay. It may not feel like much, but trust me – you've done a lot of heavy lifting!

Room to brainstorm and collect your notes and thoughts...

2. BUILDING THE STORY FOUNDATION

Room to brainstorm and collect your notes and thoughts...

THE SCREENPLAY OUTLINE WORKBOOK

Here's a space to collect everything you've figured out so far so you can see what you're working with:

Protagonist:

_____
_____
_____
_____

Story goal:

_____
_____
_____
_____

Protagonist's external stakes:

_____
_____
_____
_____

Protagonist's internal stakes:

_____
_____
_____
_____

2. BUILDING THE STORY FOUNDATION

Antagonist or opposition:

_____
_____
_____
_____

Antagonist's goal:

_____
_____
_____
_____

Antagonist's external stakes, if applicable, and internal stakes (optional):

_____
_____
_____
_____

And now you can take a moment to celebrate your progress. Then? It's back to the screenplay!

Once you have all of the foundation pieces figured out, one optional but helpful exercise can be writing a logline. A logline is just a one-sentence summary or encapsulation of your story. Writing a logline requires a low investment of time and effort and can be a great momentum builder. With just one sentence, you begin to shape your story.

Take a look at these logline examples for existing movies, noting how each one contains or at least indicates each of the foundation elements. (I've called them out for you in the first example.) Then, try to logline your own story.

Safe House, written by David Guggenheim

A CIA field officer struggles to take his prisoner, a former CIA agent-gone-rogue, four miles to a safe house with an assortment of bad guys out to get them.

(For example: protagonist = "a CIA field officer," goal = "take his prisoner to a safe house," antagonist = "an assortment of bad guys," stakes = implied in the "bad guys out to get them" and we can also assume the field officer's job may be at stake since this is a professional task.)

The Ring, screenplay by Ehren Kruger, based on the novel by Koji Suzuki

When a single mom watches a cursed videotape, she has seven days to solve the mystery and stop the curse before it kills her.

Hell or High Water, written by Taylor Sheridan

Facing foreclosure of his family's farm, a divorced father and his ex-con brother team for a skillfully-calculated bank robbing spree that puts them on a collision course with two Texas Rangers determined to take them down.

2. BUILDING THE STORY FOUNDATION

Lars and the Real Girl, written by Nancy Oliver

A grieving and delusional young man strikes up an unconventional relationship with a blowup sex doll and struggles to continue the romance despite his brother's disapproval.

Jaws, screenplay by Peter Benchley and Carl Gottlieb, based on the novel by Peter Benchley

When a killer great white shark begins to menace his small island community, the new police chief sets out to protect the town before more lives are lost.

◆

Ready to give it a try?

Start by writing down your foundation elements, then simply arrange them into one sentence, adjusting the order and language to try out different variations.

And for more in-depth information and instruction on writing loglines, look for my (free) ebook, *Logline Shortcuts: Unlock your story and pitch your screenplay in one simple sentence.*

SECTION 3

Finding the Shape of the Story With 3-Act Structure

The Central Dramatic Question

Answering the CDQ

CDQ examples

What's your CDQ?

The Purpose of Each Act

3-act examples

Brainstorm what happens in each act of your screenplay

Finding the Shape of the Story With 3-Act Structure

Within the entertainment industry, movies are most often discussed in the context of three-act structure. If you're brand new to screenwriting this might feel overwhelming, but don't panic – it's not that complicated. Or, at least, it doesn't have to be.

In this section we'll cover all the basics you need to know, starting with this high-level overview:

ACT 1	ACT 2	ACT 3
25%	50%	25%

The image above is the timeline of your screenplay or movie. For the sake of simplicity, let's say your script is 100 pages. (Industry standard is generally anywhere in the 85-120 range.)

Act 1 is approximately the first quarter of your script. (25 pages or so.) Act 2 is approximately the middle 50% of your script. (From page 26 – 75 or so.) And Act 3 is approximately the last 25% of your script. (Pages 76 – 100 or so.)

Note: These numbers are *approximate*. There is no page that anything *must* happen on. The story has to entertain and move the audience – that's most important. So consider these guidelines to aim for, not rules that must be adhered to or a checklist that can be ticked off to ensure success.

The Central Dramatic Question

In the Foundations section we talked about how stories really come down to "someone wants something badly and goes after it against strong opposition." That's what the audience is tracking over the course of the screenplay: whether the protagonist will achieve the story goal or not.

The Central Dramatic Question (CDQ, or sometimes called the Major Dramatic Question / MDQ) is another way to think about that essential core of your story. It's a version of the "someone wants something" elements, but posed as a question. "Someone wants something badly – will they get it?"

- Will the boy get the girl?
- Will the brothers get the money to the bank on time?
- Will the woman catch the serial killer?

The CDQ acts like the track of a rollercoaster ride you're taking your audience on. Without the track, that ride would be directionless and ultimately not that satisfying. It forms the track or spine of the story because the whole movie is about how the CDQ will be answered. Every plot point refers back to that question.

The CDQ is formed by the end of Act One. In Act Two, plot events (conflict and obstacles!) call into question whether the protagonist will succeed. The audience roots for the protagonist and tracks their progress as the protagonist goes after their goal. By Act Three, the audience wants the answer.

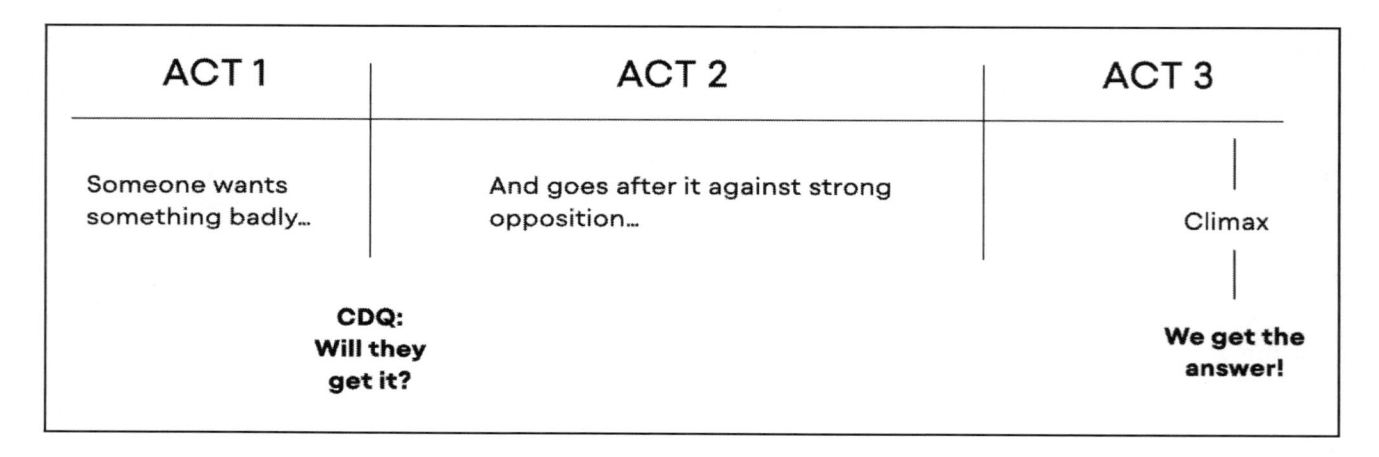

ACT 1	ACT 2	ACT 3
Someone wants something badly...	And goes after it against strong opposition...	Climax
	CDQ: Will they get it?	We get the answer!

Answering the CDQ

The Climax in Act Three (more on this in Section 5) shows the protagonist's final confrontation with the primary force of opposition. It's the battle that determines the outcome of the war, once and for all. It also answers the question – the CDQ – that the audience has been tracking through the movie:

- No, the boy doesn't get the girl.
- Yes, the brothers get the money to the bank on time.
- Yes, the woman catches the serial killer.

Once the Central Dramatic Question is answered, the movie is basically over. There's probably a bit of wrapping up to do, but too much will test the audience's patience. Because when the question they've been tracking throughout the movie has finally been answered, it feels like the story is done. We've seen what we came to see, we don't need to see much more.

So the audience wants you to close that loop that was opened when the question was formed in Act 1 – that's what they're waiting for. But in addition to that, the best endings often throw in something we didn't see coming.

As screenwriter William Goldman and screenwriting guru Robert McKee have said, respectively, endings should be "satisfying and surprising" and "inevitable and unexpected." So:

- No, the boy doesn't get the girl – *but* here comes another, and maybe she's "The One."
- Yes, the brothers get the money to the bank on time – *but* one of them dies before the task is complete.
- Yes, the woman catches the serial killer – *but* another serial killer goes free in the process.

This extra "but..." might say something about the theme, it might add a little irony for entertainment value, or it might be a way to deliver the desired emotional experience before the lights come up.

CDQ examples

Die Hard

> Will John McClane save the hostages (including his wife)?
> The answer: Yes, he does – and he stops the terrorists/thieves in the process.

The Silence of the Lambs

> Will Clarice Starling catch serial killer Buffalo Bill?
> The answer: Yes, she does – but another serial killer goes free.

Finding Dory

> Will Dory find her family?
> The answer: Yes, she does – but she realizes her friends are her family, too, and she brings everyone together in the end.

Silver Linings Playbook

> Will Pat win back his ex-wife?
> The answer: No, he doesn't – but he realizes who the right girl is for him and wins her over instead.

Back to the Future

> Will Marty McFly find a way to return to 1985?
> The answer: Yes, he does – but it's a new, improved version of his 1985, thanks to his actions in the past.

What's your CDQ?

Stating the CDQ for your screenplay might be as easy as turning the "who wants what" into a question, like in the examples above.

If you're struggling a bit to narrow in on the CDQ, try these additional prompts:

- What goal does the protagonist begin pursuing at the Break into Act 2?
- What is your protagonist ultimately trying to achieve in the movie?
- What problem is your protagonist trying to solve by going on the journey of this story?
- Who or what must your protagonist defeat or stop in order to "save the day"?

Room to brainstorm from these prompts:

_____
_____
_____
_____
_____
_____
_____
_____
_____

3. FINDING THE SHAPE OF THE STORY

_____
_____
_____
_____
_____
_____
_____

Turn your answers into questions, i.e. "Will protagonist defeat X?" Identify the question (or combine answers to form one) that encapsulates what your audience should be invested in and rooting for as they watch your movie.

Your screenplay's CDQ:

_____
_____
_____
_____

The Purpose of Each Act

Each of the three acts has a purpose, a function in the story, and when taken all together they create a satisfying experience for the audience.

Act 1 is set up. It gives us the context we need to understand the story that's about to unfold before us. In other words, it establishes who wants what and what they're up against. By the end of Act 1, the CDQ has been asked: Will X achieve Y? (That'll make sense if you read the section above.)

Act 2 is escalation, where the main thrust of the story plays out. This is where we see the "who" going after the "what" that they want, and runninginto all of the stuff that's standing in their way – the conflict and obstacles.

Act 3 is resolution. It shows us the protagonist's final push to get what they want, the climactic confrontation, and the outcome of the main conflict. Who wins, who loses. Who gets what they want, who doesn't. Or maybe, who gets something unexpected that suits them better.

3-act examples

In *Finding Dory*:

Act 1 sets up that Dory, a fish with memory issues, wants to find her long-lost parents, the family she almost forgot she had. She gets clues leading her to their location – the Morro Bay Aquarium – but she'll have to find her way in, and find her way around in order to locate them. Her memory loss makes this even harder.

CDQ: Will Dory find her family?

Act 2 shows Dory pursuing her goal: trying to find her family. Separated from her friends Marlin and Nemo, Dory struggles to navigate the big, confusing aquarium alone, but gets help from some of the aquarium residents she encounters.

Act 3 shows Dory realizing that her family isn't just her long-lost parents, but also the friends – new and old – who have supported her and believed in her, even when she didn't believe in herself. Dory masterminds a plan to help her friends break out of the aquarium and unites everyone in one big happy family.

In *The Silence of the Lambs*:

Act 1 sets up that Clarice Starling is an ambitious but inexperienced FBI trainee who gets an opportunity to help out on the investigation into serial killer Buffalo Bill, but it brings her into contact with another serial killer, Hannibal Lecter.

CDQ: Will Clarice catch the serial killer Buffalo Bill?

Act 2 shows Clarice pursuing her goal: trying to catch Buffalo Bill. To have any hope of capturing him, Clarice must figure out his real identity. So Clarice enlists Hannibal's help, but is forced to match wits with Hannibal in order to gain access to his insight and information.

Act 3 shows Clarice, having lost her access to Hannibal, following the clues on her own and finally figuring out Bill's true identity. When she does she must face off with him, managing to bring down the serial killer and save the latest victim.

Brainstorm what happens in each act of your screenplay

With the function of each act in mind, we can take the "someone wants something" statement (or a logline, if you have one) and break the story idea down into its three major parts.

3. FINDING THE SHAPE OF THE STORY

⋄ Act 1 is context, it sets up what the protagonist wants to do (the story goal).
⋄ Act 2 is conflict and escalation, it shows the protagonist pursuing their goal and encountering opposition and obstacles.
⋄ Act 3 is resolution, it shows the protagonist confronting and resolving the main conflict. They achieve the goal or not, and we get an answer to the Central Dramatic Question.

At this point we're aiming for broad strokes descriptions; a paragraph or so for each act of your story. If you're feeling stuck, try these prompts to help you flesh out each section:

Act 1: Set up the story goal

⋄ Who do we need to pay attention to? (the protagonist)
⋄ What problem are they going to try to solve or what goal are they going to try to achieve by the end of this movie? (goal)
⋄ Why is this important to them? (stakes)
⋄ What's the main thing creating conflict for them? (opposition)

_____
_____
_____
_____
_____
_____
_____
_____

Act 2: Escalate the conflict

⋄ What does the protagonist do to pursue their goal?
⋄ What does the antagonist or main force of opposition do to pursue their goal or oppose the protagonist's goal?
⋄ How do things get harder along the way?
⋄ How do things get more important or urgent along the way?

Act 3: Resolve the main conflict

- What new method or strategy does the protagonist have to try in order to finally achieve their goal?
- What's the final confrontation or battle to be won before they can declare a success?
- Do they solve their problem or achieve their goal?
- Describe the outcome.

3. FINDING THE SHAPE OF THE STORY

_____
_____
_____
_____
_____
_____

With the functions of each act in mind, write out your story's three-act summary here:

Act 1: _____
_____
_____
_____
_____
_____
_____
_____

CDQ:_____
_____
_____
_____
_____

Act 2: _____

_____

_____

_____

_____

_____

_____

_____

_____

_____

Act 3: _____

_____

_____

_____

_____

_____

_____

_____

_____

_____

3. FINDING THE SHAPE OF THE STORY

Room to brainstorm and collect your notes and thoughts...

SECTION 4

Developing the Main Character

Transformation

Transformation examples

Transformation and Theme

The "What I've learned…" exercise

Matching character arc to plot

Transformation brainstorm

Defining Characteristic

Defining characteristic examples

Defining characteristic brainstorm

The Protagonist's Introduction

Getting us hooked on the protagonist

Protagonist introduction brainstorm

Introducing your protagonist

Have a character but no plot?

Developing the Main Character

Earlier in this workbook we talked about how to identify the protagonist of your story, and now is a good time to flesh out that character a bit more.

The protagonist is the character we spend the most time with, arguably the most important character in your screenplay. They're also the one you'll probably get to know the most in writing your story.

Understanding the protagonist from the inside out will make your job of writing them easier, but it can be overwhelming to think about creating a whole, realistically complex character from scratch. So instead of trying to know everything, we'll start with two aspects of the protagonist that can do much of the heavy lifting in your screenplay.

Transformation

Most movies are about a transformation of some kind. Usually it's a change in the protagonist, although sometimes the change is in the world around the protagonist.

Why are movies about transformation? We're drawn to stories of change because change indicates consequence, which conveys meaning. If there's no change in a story, then it feels like the events of the story didn't matter; they were inconsequential.

The change in a character over the course of a story is their character arc, which is what we'll focus on in this section.

Do all protagonists arc? No.

But if you look closely you'll see that most main characters change in some way, even if it's small, especially in mainstream movies. Movies tend to be about transformative experiences, and most often we gauge the impact of the story's events by how the protagonist has been affected.

The protagonist's transformation also doesn't have to be a huge change or complete 180. In fact, smaller shifts can feel more realistic, attainable, and relatable. When a character gains a hard-won new understanding that helps them lead a better or more fulfilling life, it can be emotionally engaging – no matter how seemingly small the actual change.

Transformation examples

In *About A Boy*, protagonist Will goes from responsibility-phobic single guy, to someone who is happy to have real, meaningful relationships.

In *Bridesmaids*, protagonist Annie goes from someone who is stuck in a life rut but afraid to take action to change it, to someone who accepts change and is willing to go for what she wants.

In *Finding Dory*, protagonist Dory goes from feeling vulnerable and handicapped by her memory issues, to feeling confident in her own special abilities.

Transformation and Theme

It's useful to note that the nature of the character's transformation also indicates the story's theme. A movie's theme is its takeaway message or meaning. It's whatever universal lesson or philosophical idea or value-based argument the story as a whole imparts to the audience.

For example:

In *Little Miss Sunshine* we might take away the message that life is about being yourself, not winning the approval others.

In *Hell or High Water*, the movie's specific point of view is: life is a struggle and in order to survive, one must be willing to fight to the death.

In *Bridesmaids* the idea is that fighting change will only keep you stuck. If you want to be happy you have to accept that change happens and go toward the life you want.

A movie doesn't have to have an obvious theme in order to work, but a compelling theme helps your story connect with and move an audience. Your movie or screenplay becomes more than entertainment; it becomes a meaningful experience.

And for the writer, theme can serve as the organizing principle of your story. Every element and story choice you make should add to the same thematic argument or exploration of a thematic idea. I like to think of it as your screenplay having one conversation about one thing.

How does theme relate to character? At the root of the character's transformation is a lesson or shift in worldview, and that lesson is essentially the theme of the movie. The

4. DEVELOPING THE MAIN CHARACTER

way the story plays out as a whole "proves" the theme for the audience.

If stories are guides for life and the theme is the takeaway lesson about how to navigate it, then it makes sense that we'd see the theme demonstrated in how the protagonist adapts or changes over the course of the story.

ACT 1	ACT 2	ACT 3
Character demonstrates their current or "old" worldview or way of being.	Character learns the thematic lesson.	Character demonstrates the new, transformed worldview or way of being.

The "What I've learned…" exercise

Ready for a break? Let's take the theoretical stuff and make it more concrete and practical. This exercise is a chance to do some fun, no-pressure writing, connect with your main character, and narrow in on the message at the heart of your story.

Toward the end of a movie (and the end of the character's arc), you'll often see the protagonist state what they've learned from the experience we've just watched. They tell us the lesson or realization they've now embraced. Sometimes it's one line of dialogue, other times it's a whole speech. Not in every movie, of course, but it happens a lot.

For example, in the movie *The DUFF*, protagonist Bianca goes from being someone who feels like she needs to change herself when she learns she's considered the "Designated Ugly Fat Friend" in her group, to someone who accepts herself exactly the way she is. (And ultimately gets the boy next door, Wesley, who happens to date Bianca's nemesis, Madison.)

Bianca's transformed state is on full display at the Homecoming dance, when she finally confronts Madison. Here, we see Bianca's "What I've learned…" speech:

> "Madison, you used to make me so upset. But now I just feel bad for you. Yeah, I'm somebody's DUFF. Guess what – so are you. So is everybody. There's always gonna be somebody prettier, or more talented, or richer than you. But it shouldn't affect how you see yourself. You label everybody to try to keep them down, but you end up missing out on all this great stuff around you. You have Wesley and

you treat him like he's stupid, but he isn't. People don't like him because he's with you – they like him because he's an amazing guy. Look, I like myself. I wouldn't want to be anybody else. And I realize now that none of this matters to me. But it does to you. It's your dream. And I totally support that. Just don't tear me down for not [caring] about your labels because in the end, they're meaningless."

Now it's your turn! For this exercise, think about the transformation your protagonist goes through in your movie, and the lesson they must embrace in order to reach that transformed state.

Then, write a speech the protagonist might give in which they tell us what they've learned from this experience. They could be talking to their antagonist, or to a love interest or mentor, or even a stadium full of people. Or you could imagine the protagonist speaking directly to the audience, either in voice over or by breaking the fourth wall.

You don't need to decide exactly how the scene will play out. This exercise is about exploring what the protagonist would say once they've gone through the transformative experience. Once they were out the other side and could see what they needed to change and how they're a better version of themselves now.

And it's okay if you don't know how to precisely or concisely explain the lesson yet. Don't worry about getting it "right" or perfect on the first try. If you write from the protagonist's point of view and let yourself ramble on the page, I think you'll find yourself circling the point you really want to make.

Put yourself in the protagonist's shoes. Let your imagination go, and write what comes to mind when you think about how your protagonist is wiser, stronger, healthier, or happier by the end of the movie.

_____

_____

_____

_____

_____

_____

_____

_____

4. DEVELOPING THE MAIN CHARACTER

Matching character arc to plot

Just as important as showing the transformation itself, is showing *how* the transformation occurs as a direct result of the plot.

In any good story, plot and character development are intertwined. Plot events act on a character and force change. The changing character makes choices that drive plot direction.

Very simply, a character may start out as one sort of person and gradually transform into a different sort of person as they experience the events of the plot. In that way, plot and character arc go hand-in-hand.

When we can see how the experience causes the protagonist's specific change, then the transformation feels earned, the story feels more meaningful, and the audience is satisfied.

There are three parts that the audience needs to see in order to understand the complete character arc:

◇ In Act 1, we need to see a character who in some way needs the transformation.
◇ In Act 2, we need to see how the events the character experiences press on that need and cause the change.
◇ In Act 3, we need to see the character's resulting transformed state.

ACT 1	ACT 2	ACT 3
We see a protagonist who in some way needs the transformation.	What the protagonist experiences in Act 2 presses on that need and causes the character to recognize the thematic lesson.	The protagonist demonstrates their transformation.

Transformation brainstorm

For your story, think about what change or transformation the character experiences. And, just as importantly, how do the events of the plot cause that change?

Remember to consider all three parts of the character arc. For example, in the movie *The Silence of the Lambs*:

4. DEVELOPING THE MAIN CHARACTER

In Act 1, a character who in some way needs the transformation:

Clarice Starling secretly fears she's not capable of "saving the lambs," i.e. the innocents who need help. She wants to stop bad things from happening but she doesn't know if she has what it takes (and fears she doesn't). If she doesn't overcome this insecurity, she'll likely fail in her career and life mission.

In Act 2, the events the character experiences press on that need and cause the change:

As Clarice navigates the world of men in which she is an underdog, and as she matches wits with Hannibal Lecter, her confidence grows. By the end of Act 2 she is forced to go it alone, relying on her own abilities and what she's learned from Hannibal to solve the case on her own.

In Act 3, the character's resulting transformed state:

Clarice works the clues and figures out Buffalo Bill's identity. She's solved the case. And when she ends up facing off with Buffalo Bill without backup, she is able to bring him down and prove she is capable of "saving the lambs."

Your turn! Brainstorm how the transformation will show up in the three parts of the character's arc:

In Act 1, a character who in some way needs the transformation:

_____
_____
_____
_____
_____
_____
_____
_____
_____
_____

In Act 2, the events the character experiences press on that need and cause the change:

_____
_____
_____
_____
_____
_____
_____
_____
_____

In Act 3, the character's resulting transformed state:

_____
_____
_____
_____
_____
_____
_____
_____
_____

Defining Characteristic

Some writers like to do lengthy character bios to get to know their protagonists (and other characters). If that's you, great. If not, I suggest identifying the one defining characteristic that's most important for this character in this story.

While you might have heard that a protagonist needs a "flaw," the defining characteristic doesn't have to be an objectively negative quality. An effective defining characteristic is just a behavior or strategy that's not serving the character as well as they think. It's a survival strategy which is about to run out of usefulness to the character even though they probably don't realize it.

It is, however, useful to choose an *active* defining characteristic for the protagonist. Something we can see in their behavior. That'll make it easier to show the characteristic in the screenplay.

And keep in mind we're talking about the defining quality *when we meet the character*. It defines who they are at the start of the story, before they've gone through the transformational experience, and this trait may be exactly what changes over the course of the story.

Defining characteristic examples

In *Die Hard*, John McClane is macho and uncompromising when we meet him. It's his way or the highway. It's not a healthy strategy, but that's good — at the start of the story. Because it gives him room to grow. Over the course of this movie he'll come to realize that his behavior needs to change if he's going to have a happy marriage.

In *The Silence of the Lambs*, Clarice Starling is ambitious. This defines her actions when we meet her. It's not an objectively negative quality, and it's not one that will change or even needs to change by the end of the movie. Clarice will probably always be ambitious. But at the start of the movie her ambition outweighs her confidence. And she will always be dissatisfied (and probably unsuccessful) if she doesn't also gain the confidence to do her job well.

In *Bridesmaids*, Annie's pretending she's satisfied with life as it is — or, basically, lying to herself. She pretends all she wants from love interest Ted is a booty call, even though that kind of non-relationship makes her feel bad about herself. She pretends she's okay with her terrible roommate situation. She pretends she's nothing but happy for Lillian's engagement when there's a part of her that's freaking out about what this means for their friendship. Eventually Annie will see that pretending she's happy isn't serving her, as it keeps her stuck in the same rut.

Defining characteristic brainstorm

The protagonist's defining characteristic is related to the character arc, which – like so much else – connects back to the story's theme. (Because really, everything in your screenplay connects back to the theme, or the meaning at the heart of the story.)

With that in mind, here are two ways to brainstorm options for the protagonist's defining characteristic:

1. Brainstorm defining characteristic from character arc

For example, if your screenplay is, at its core, about a character who goes from being stuck in a life rut to one who embraces change and goes for what they want, then you can use that starting point to brainstorm possible defining characteristics.

What behavior might someone who is "stuck in a life rut" display?

Maybe they're an addict, escaping through drugs or alcohol. Maybe they're a busybody, focusing on other people in order to ignore their own problems. Or, maybe they're lying and pretending everything's okay just the way it is even though they're truly unhappy.

Brainstorm some possibilities and then choose the one that makes the most sense for your story.

For your story, what's the transformation? State it as "From X to Y" here:

_____

_____

_____

What behavior might someone who is at the "X" starting point display? Brainstorm the possibilities:

_____

_____

_____

_____

_____

4. DEVELOPING THE MAIN CHARACTER

Which one makes the most sense for your story? For the tone and genre of your screenplay? And which one makes you excited to write that character?

_____

_____

_____

_____

_____

2. Brainstorm defining characteristic from theme

If you know what the theme of your story is, that can lead you to the character arc, and then to the defining characteristic as outlined above.

And that's because character arc and theme are so inextricably linked. Generally, the theme is the lesson at the heart of the character's transformation. The way the story plays out proves the theme. We understand the meaning or point of the story – the theme – through the way the character changes and how the plot resolves.

If the path of the character's transformation looks like this:

Needs Lesson → Learns Thematic Lesson → Becomes happier, healthier person

Then you can fill in what you know and solve for what you don't.

For example, say the theme you want to express with your story is, "No man is an island." You know the path of transformation will look like this:

[Starting point X, needs lesson] → Learns "No man is an island." → Becomes person who has real, meaningful relationships.

Solve for X by brainstorming:

Who needs to learn that "no man is an island"? Who isn't already experiencing real, meaningful relationships with others? Or, who cannot or will not cultivate real, meaningful relationships?

Maybe…

Someone who is a shut in.
Someone who is agoraphobic.
A misanthrope.
An unreliable slacker.
A fiercely independent, responsibility-phobic single guy.

As before, choose the one that makes the most sense for the story, and the tone and genre of the screenplay you're writing.

What theme do you want to express with your story?

_____
_____
_____
_____

Write out your protagonist's path of transformation here using the template:

X, Needs Lesson → Learns Thematic Lesson → Becomes happier, healthier person

4. DEVELOPING THE MAIN CHARACTER

Solve for X by brainstorming:

- Who needs the thematic lesson?
- Who isn't already living as or experiencing the happier, healthier endpoint?
- Who cannot or will not, for whatever reason, live life in that happier, healthier way?

Try to write your options in terms of an active characteristic or behavior as in the example above, i.e. agoraphobic, unreliable, or responsibility-phobic.

_____
_____
_____
_____
_____
_____
_____
_____

Which one makes the most sense for your story? For the tone and genre of your screenplay? And which one makes you excited to write that character?

_____
_____
_____
_____
_____
_____
_____
_____

The Protagonist's Introduction

All of the big-picture thinking we've been doing is valuable (necessary, even!) but you might be feeling antsy to really get into the on-the-page writing work. Or you might be feeling the need to re-ignite your attraction for your story by coming up with a specific scene that you love and can't wait to see in your movie.

So let's take a moment to zoom in on one key moment in your screenplay: the protagonist's introduction.

We've discussed why the protagonist is such an important character, and our first introduction to him or her carries a lot of weight. As an audience, one of the first things we do when we enter a story is try to figure out who our vehicle is, who we're going to ride along with through this experience.

The protagonist's introduction directs the audience's attention and helps to orient the reader, making it clear whose story this is, who we're going to follow and root for, who we should invest our emotions in.

No pressure, right? Don't worry – in the next section we'll brainstorm ways to introduce your protagonist so that the audience can't wait to follow them into the story.

Getting us hooked on the protagonist

Whether it's a classic hero or someone we'll love to hate, the story's protagonist must be compelling in some way. Protagonists don't have to be likable, but they do have to engage us somehow. Which makes sense – a character has to be interesting enough that readers and audiences want to spend time with them, otherwise we'll move on to something that does capture our attention.

In a screenplay, there's no time to waste. We want to hook the audience from the first time they meet the protagonist. So what makes us hook into a character?

In his book *"Writing Screenplays That Sell"*, Michael Hauge outlines nine strategies that can be used to introduce a character, three that he calls essential tactics. He even goes so far as to say that one of these three *must* be employed in order for us to identify with the hero.

While I'm not a fan of hard-and-fast rules, I do think these three techniques are widely used to good effect and an excellent place to begin brainstorming how you could introduce the protagonist of your story in a way that will hook the audience. They are:

4. DEVELOPING THE MAIN CHARACTER

1. Create sympathy for the character through undeserved misfortune.

We naturally feel compassion for victims of tragedy, especially if we believe their misfortune to be through no fault of their own. That sympathy creates alignment with the character, effectively putting us on their side and priming us to root for them.

Blue Ruin is a strong example of creating sympathy through undeserved misfortune. We meet the protagonist in his current, tragic state and then quickly learn about the horrible events that caused his life to go off the rails.

2. Create worry for the character by putting them in jeopardy.

Jeopardy is the threat of danger, and thinking broadly about different types of danger can help you come up with many options in this category. The threat of capture, exposure, embarrassment, or defeat can all be effective, depending on the tone of the movie.

An example is the movie *Everly*. It opens on a shell-shocked, half-naked young woman limping into a hotel bathroom. Men's voices are heard from outside the door. Danger looms.

3. Make the character likable.

Wait— didn't I say we wouldn't worry about likability?

To be clear, your protagonist doesn't *have* to be likable. But it is an option, and often a good one. When we like a character we're much more willing to go along for the ride they're on.

However, "likeable" doesn't mean inoffensive to the point of blandness. It's not about flying under the radar; there has to be something about the character that we're drawn to, that causes us to actively like them.

As Michael Hauge says: "There are basically three ways to get a reader to like your hero, which can be used singly or in combination," and they are:

- Make the character a good or nice person (young Officer Hoyt in *Training Day*)
- Make the character funny (*Deadpool*)
- Make the character good at what he does (*Baby Driver* for example, or even Cassandra in *Promising Young Woman*)

Protagonist introduction brainstorm

Brainstorm all the options you can think of for using these techniques in your protagonist introduction. No need to come up with whole scenes right now. Instead, think about how each of the techniques might play out in a moment or a situation. Later you can decide which one, or even combine several, to use in the introductory scene.

1. Undeserved misfortune:

What could we see happen to the protagonist (or learn has happened in the past) that would make us feel sympathy for them?

_____
_____
_____
_____
_____
_____
_____
_____
_____
_____

2. Jeopardy:

What threat of danger or other negative event could we see looming before the protagonist, which would make us worry about their physical (or even psychological) safety?

_____
_____
_____
_____

4. DEVELOPING THE MAIN CHARACTER

_____
_____
_____
_____
_____
_____
_____

3. Likability:

Are they a good or nice person? In what way? How might we see this in action?

_____
_____
_____
_____
_____
_____

Are they funny? In what way, and how can we see it on screen?

_____
_____
_____
_____
_____
_____
_____

Are they good at what they do? What job, skill, or talent could the protagonist demonstrate? Bonus points if it's unusual or not many can do it at the same level.

_____
_____
_____
_____
_____
_____

Introducing your protagonist

Now that you've brainstormed possibilities using each of the techniques, think about how you can showcase one (or combine several) in a scene in which we meet your protagonist for the first time:

_____
_____
_____
_____
_____
_____
_____
_____
_____
_____
_____
_____

4. DEVELOPING THE MAIN CHARACTER

Have a character but no plot?

Some projects start with concept, others start with theme, others start from character. No matter where you begin, you have to figure all of it out eventually.

But fortunately, in the same way you can "do the math" to find a defining behavior that works with a particular theme or character arc (as we did in the previous section), so can you use what you know about one element of a story to find others that you don't yet know.

(That's because everything in a screenplay is related and interdependent, creating one big, tightly woven story tapestry.)

No matter where you start, ultimately you have to answer the question: "What story do I want to tell?" And every choice should connect to and create that same story.

It sounds so simple. We answer that question with every project we develop. But it's sometimes hard to answer, and can be particularly so when you're starting a project from character instead of concept.

So if you're in that spot now, here are some questions to help you find the plot:

1. Can you get in touch with an arc of transformation that interests you?

I say "that interests you" as a reminder. Often writers want to find the "right" answer to whatever story choice they're facing. When actually, most of the choices you face come down to what draws your interest, what rings true to you, and – yes – what story you want to tell.

If you're unsure, doing some free-writing on your idea is a good place to start. In your free-writing, look for clues that can be jumping-off points.

You might come up with a character description like this, for example: "She sees herself as an outsider, someone who doesn't belong." And if we know this about her, we can think of possible character arcs. Such as…

> That description could be the character's starting point. Then she could change from "outsider loner" into someone who does belong, someone who has a place amongst a group of friends or people united in some other way.

> Or, maybe that character's view of herself as someone who doesn't belong means she starts the story desperate to fit in and constantly seeking approval. And then maybe she becomes a person who accepts herself and who doesn't need validation from others.

4. DEVELOPING THE MAIN CHARACTER

These are just two options. Take some time to brainstorm all the potential arcs you can think of based on what you know about your character. Choose one that sparks your interest and feels right, and then move forward.

Using the example above, you might decide the character's arc is, "from desperate people-pleaser to confident, independent woman."

Then you can think about...

2. What external events could cause that change?

You might have some other story elements in mind at this point, so you can start examining those or begin to brainstorm from scratch. Think about what kinds of events could cause the transformation you've decided to explore.

If you already have a world in mind, for example, you could think about how the circumstances of that world, or events that would be likely to happen in it, would put pressure on your character and cause them to change.

For our example, let's say our story world involves a particular niche community, and we like the idea of the character entering this niche community somehow.

With that in mind, we can begin to think about how entering the niche community could cause the transformation we've decided to explore. ("From desperate people-pleaser to confident, independent woman," the character arc chosen above.)

And we could come up with some options:

> Maybe the character does everything to try to fit in with the new group but they just keep demanding more and more, and over time she realizes how much she's hurting herself and/or her family and she finds the strength to walk away.

> Maybe she becomes a target of this niche community, who are all violent types. And the protagonist has to fight them off, through which she learns she's undeniably strong and can clearly take care of herself all by herself, so she doesn't need anyone's approval.

> Maybe she's a desperate people-pleaser in her regular life, but when she discovers this niche community, she gets an opportunity to turn the tables and demand other people please her. And maybe she loses herself more and more until she realizes she's lost everything that truly mattered in order to be a part of this group. Finally she'll have to stand up for herself, create boundaries, and extricate herself from these unhealthy relationships.

The three examples above are all different stories. The shape, the structure, the big thematic idea at the center. There may be some overlap in events or characters or moments, but they're each a unique story that would be plotted out a different way.

If you can't tell where these ideas are coming from, I'm simply thinking of ways that the events of the plot could cause the transformation we decided on for the protagonist. Just the broad strokes that tell us what the story is.

Once you generate a bunch of possible stories, you can look for that spark of inspiration or recognition. Let your attention be drawn to what interests or inspires you. You want to identify which story you want to tell with this script. That's the big question to guide your choices.

So brainstorm all the options you can think of and then choose just one, at least for now. Whatever it is, whatever version you like and that feels right to you, that gives you the big arc of your story.

From there, you can figure out the specifics of that story. You'll plot out the sequence of external events and experiences that create the desired emotional journey and transformation. All from the character you started with.

Room to brainstorm and collect your notes and thoughts...

4. DEVELOPING THE MAIN CHARACTER

Room to brainstorm and collect your notes and thoughts...

SECTION 5

Creating the Screenplay's Framework with Six Major Plot Points

What Are the Major Plot Points?

How to Know Where a Plot Event Should Go

Functions of the Major Plot Points

Inciting Incident

Break into Act 2

Midpoint

Low Point*

Break into Act 3

Climax*

Figuring Out Your Story's Major Plot Points

Major Plot Points Examples

Major Plot Points Brainstorm

Creating the Screenplay's Framework with Six Major Plot Points

Before we continue, take a moment to think about what you've accomplished so far. Be proud. You've made great progress building the foundation of your story and fleshing out the character who will be our guide through the experience.

Now let's start to give form to the story by identifying the Major Plot Points. These six story points are significant because together they determine the overall shape of the story.

If we're getting technical, the six Major Plot Points are made up of four plot *points* and two additional sections of the plot that are useful to include in order to get a big-picture view of the entire story. But that's splitting hairs a bit; let's agree they're important points in the plot and get to the useful stuff.

What are plot points? How do they function? And how do you know which plot points are major or otherwise?

The plot is the sequence of events in your story, in which we track a character's pursuit of a goal or objective. A plot point is an event that changes the character's orientation to that objective.

At each plot point, the character is either closer to or farther from the goal. In that way, plot points mark progress and move the story forward.

The major plot points are plot points just the same, but they have more specific and specialized functions. And the major plot points work together to create a spine for the story.

What Are the Major Plot Points?

There's probably some debate about what's considered a major plot point but the ones that will be most useful to you in figuring out your story right now are:

- Inciting Incident
- Break into Act 2
- Midpoint
- Low Point*
- Break into Act 3
- Climax*

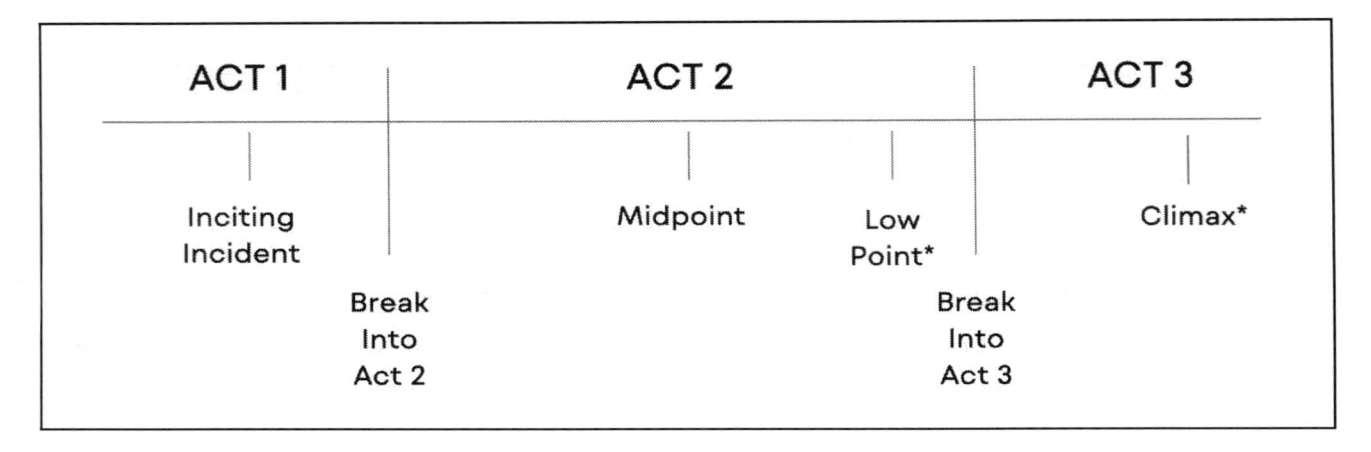

```
        ACT 1          |        ACT 2          |        ACT 3

    Inciting                  Midpoint    Low              Climax*
    Incident                              Point*
                Break                            Break
                Into                             Into
                Act 2                            Act 3
```

You may be used to calling these plot points by different names, and that's okay too. What you call each one is less important than your understanding of the purpose and function.

Together, these plot points give you a high-level view of the entire story. They give us a feel for the whole shape of it even if we don't know every detail just yet.

*Note: The two I've marked with asterisks may not technically occur in a single plot event and are more likely to play out over several plot points instead. But they are important pieces of the big picture nonetheless so it'll be helpful to figure them out at this point in the process too.

Even if you don't think of yourself as a "plotter," figuring out these big story milestones can be a useful part of your process. Having targets to aim for along the way provides a sense of direction so you're not just writing blindly, and breaking the bigger project into smaller chunks (delineated by the major plot points) can make writing it feel more manageable.

How to Know Where a Plot Event Should Go

A question I get a lot in my screenwriting workshops and in one-on-one consulting is: where "should" a particular plot event go?

Is this where the kiss should go? Should the protagonist meet his big rival here? Or here? Is this where the big secret should be revealed? Or should that happen earlier? Is this where I have to show the antagonist?

And the answer is almost always, "It depends." (Which writers don't like the sound of, but is absolutely true.)

Where something "should" go in your story depends on what you're trying to achieve with it. It depends on what function you're trying to fulfill by planting that plot event at a given place in the story.

For example, to answer the question, "Is this where the kiss should go?" we need to know what you're trying to achieve with that kiss.

- ◇ Are you trying to cement the stakes for the protagonist, the thing that will motivate her to go on this adventure in the first place?
- ◇ Or are you trying to prove that he's the wrong guy, and she should actually be pursing this other boy-next-door who's been waiting in the wings for her to notice him?
- ◇ Or something else entirely?

A kiss is just a kiss until it means something. In your story, a kiss might have any number of different purposes. Because of that, it could occur at any number of different places in the plot. It just depends on what you want it to do.

Functions of the Major Plot Points

When I'm working with writers on their story's major turning points, I always encourage them to know what they're trying to achieve first and then to find the event that accomplishes that purpose.

Let's look at each major plot point's function in the story so you can identify your own.

Inciting Incident

Also known as the Catalyst (if you're a *Save the Cat!* fan), this plot point usually occurs about 10–15 pages into the script, and you might think of it as the event that sets the story into motion or that shakes up the protagonist's normal world.

It is usually something that happens *to* the protagonist (as opposed to a choice or action *by* the protagonist). Often it's the first appearance or indication of the antagonist or main force of opposition.

The Inciting Incident's function in the story is to kick off a problem (or opportunity) that the protagonist must act on, which is how it sets the story into motion: it creates circumstances in which the protagonist *must* take action, and which soon leads to forming the story goal.

Break into Act 2

Also known as Plot Point 1 (if you're a Syd Field fan), the Break into Act 2 is the turning point between Act 1 and Act 2.

It's often described as the event that locks the protagonist into the story. What does that actually mean, though? It usually looks like the protagonist forming or declaring the story goal, or the protagonist beginning to pursue the story goal in earnest.

This plot point launches the story into Act 2 by solidifying what the protagonist is going to pursue over the course of this story. This gives the audience something to track. It helps us engage with your story, because it allows us to follow the progress toward the goal.

Midpoint

Also known as... Nope, I think that's the only name for it. You probably notice the Midpoint turn in movies without realizing it. After the Midpoint, effective stories feel more intense, faster paced, more urgent, and higher stakes, and sometimes even drastically change their direction.

The function of the Midpoint is to create new tension. It causes the audience to lean in with renewed interest or more emotional investment, or both. What happens at the Midpoint makes us eager to stick around for the rest of the story.

To fulfill that function, a good Midpoint usually does one or both of these things in a big way: raise the stakes and/or increase opposition.

Sometimes that looks like a big reveal, for the audience and/or the main character. Sometimes it's the start of a ticking clock. It can be a huge defeat or a huge win. It can be a "now it's personal" loss, or "sex at 60" moment (where a romantic relationship takes a major step).

However you decide it should manifest, the goal here is to re-engage our curiosity or interest, or to get us to re-invest emotionally, or both.

Low Point*

If you're a follower of *Save the Cat!*, the low point we're talking about here includes the All is Lost and Dark Night of the Soul story beats.

This plot point* is often described as the point where the protagonist seems furthest from reaching his or her goal. It might be where the protagonist loses their support system, such as if a mentor character dies, the love interest leaves, or the hero is fired from his position of responsibility or authority.

This is the place in the story where the character may first realize what he or she must learn or change going forward. We often see the thematic lesson reflected back to the protagonist here even if they're not ready to accept it yet.

Break into Act 3

Also known (to Syd Field fans) as Plot Point 2, this plot point marks the start of the story's resolution. Its function is to propel us into Act 3, to launch the line of action that will ultimately resolve the main conflict.

A hallmark of this plot point is the protagonist's new plan to achieve the story goal or new goal altogether. (Sometimes it also showcases the protagonist's new, "growth" way of addressing the problem — now that he or she has been through the transformative events of this story.)

The new plan, however nascent, far-fetched, or dangerous, will be the final attempt to achieve the story goal or resolve the main conflict. This gives us (the audience) something to track over the rest of the movie.

Climax*

Also known as the Final Battle, the climax is the main character's final confrontation with the primary force of opposition. This is the battle that determines the outcome of the war, once and for all. There will be no more chances. The goal will be achieved, or not. The audience will finally get the answer to the Central Dramatic Question.

And once the CDQ is answered, the movie is essentially over. We'll likely need just a bit of wrap-up to bring a feeling of closure and satisfaction. But that's about it.

Figuring Out Your Story's Major Plot Points

As you're working out your story, keep in mind that you don't have to discover these plot points in chronological order. Start with what you know, and use that to help you find the others.

Often when you're developing an idea, you'll have one or more of these plot points already in mind. Maybe you know what the big, climactic confrontation scene will be; it's what inspired the whole movie.

Or maybe you know what the main thrust of the movie is — the journey of Act 2 — and from that you can identify the Break Into Act 2, the event that launches that journey.

And if you know the Break Into Act 2, then you can brainstorm how to introduce the problem the new goal is aiming to solve. That would give you the Inciting Incident.

It's not a linear process. You'll figure out one, then do the math to figure out the others and realize you need to adjust the first one. That's okay. Soon all of the puzzle pieces will fit together. You'll be able to see the entire big picture of your screenplay living in these six plot points.

Of course, sometimes we come at stories with certain scenes already alive in our minds and we know they go somewhere, we just don't yet know where.

If you find yourself trying to slot in certain events or scenes, remember to ask yourself what purpose you need to achieve at a given point in the story, and whether your darlings do indeed achieve that effect.

The major plot points we're discussing here may show up in the majority of stories, but that doesn't mean there aren't also exceptions to the "rules". If you need to do it differently to get the effect you want, then go for it. But be deliberate about the effect you're creating with your story.

Major Plot Points Examples

Die Hard

1. **Inciting Incident:** Hans Gruber and the terrorists arrive at Nakatomi Plaza, where John McClane is trying to reconcile with his wife, Holly, during her company Christmas party. The terrorists are the problem, even though John isn't aware of them yet (though he will be shortly).

2. **Break into Act 2:** John has learned the terrorists are ruthless killers, and he's the only one who's not being held hostage, so he's the only one who can save them all. His story goal is to save the hostages (including Holly) from the terrorists.

3. **Midpoint**: Even though it looks like outside help is on the way and John thinks he can hand over responsibility, the terrorists are listening in on his communications so they have an advantage. They indicate they're coming for John so they can get the detonators they need in order to complete their plan.

4. **Low Point:** A few things combine to create a real low point for John. First, Hans and his crew have nearly broken into the vault; they have just one step left. The FBI arrives and takes over from local police, which means John's ally on the outside, Powell, loses his power to help. And then John and Hans come face to face, but Hans pretends to be a hostage – and John gives him a gun! It looks like John has made a fatal misstep...

5. **Break into Act 3:** But John's two steps ahead of Hans (and us) this time. Their battle continues into Act 3, with John a bit wiser, a bit more insightful.

6. **Climax**: John realizes what Hans's real plan is, uses that info to save the hostages, and then faces off with Hans to save wife Holly. When the movie ends, we know John has solved his problem and saved his marriage too.

Bridesmaids

1. **Inciting Incident:** Annie's best friend, Lillian, announces her engagement and asks Annie to be her Maid of Honor. Annie's new problem is wanting to hold onto her best friend, who is moving forward in life while Annie is stuck.

2. **Break into Act 2**: By the end of the engagement party, Annie has met rival Helen (as well as the other bridesmaids) and can see the challenge coming her way. Annie's story goal is to fend off Helen's attempts to show her up and take over as Maid of Honor and best friend.

3. **Midpoint**: Annie accidentally ruins the bachelorette party and Lillian tells her Helen's going to be Maid of Honor now. Annie has lost her position in the wedding, and is left struggling to hold onto her place as Lillian's best friend (raising the stakes).

4. **Low Point**: At the bridal shower, Annie tanks her friendship with Lillian and is disinvited from the wedding altogether. On the way home she also gets in a fight with love interest Officer Rhodes. She's hit rock bottom.

5. **Break into Act 3**: We see Annie begin to change her ways, saying goodbye to her booty-call Ted. It's the start of her "growth" way of navigating the story.

6. **Climax**: Annie learns Lillian, the bride, is missing. Annie tracks her down and gives her the pep talk (and dress re-design) Lillian needs in order to walk down the aisle, and Annie has repaired her friendship and is back in the wedding party. When the movie ends we know Annie has solved her problem and made changes to put her own life back on the right track.

Major Plot Points Brainstorm

Ready to brainstorm your Major Plot Points? Great!

Start with the one(s) you know. Plug them into the worksheet here and ask yourself if they fulfill the functions as needed. Then use the prompts to think about the functions of the others, how they relate back to the story goal and to each other, and "do the math" to figure out the rest of the Major Plot Points for your story.

Major Plot Points prompts:

1. **Inciting Incident:** What new problem or opportunity that *must* be dealt with is introduced into the protagonist's life?

___

2. **Break into Act 2:** What is the story goal (or plan to achieve it) that the protagonist is ready to declare? How do we know (i.e. how can you show) that the protagonist is now committed to or beginning to pursue that goal?

___

5. CREATING THE SCREENPLAY'S FRAMEWORK

3. **Midpoint:** What could happen to increase the opposition and/or raise the stakes in a major way? Does this event send the story in an entirely new direction, and if so – how?

_____
_____
_____
_____
_____
_____
_____
_____
_____
_____

4. **Low Point:** What does being on the verge of failure or hitting rock bottom look like to the protagonist? Think in relation to the story goal and stakes. What would be the worst that could happen, and how can it appear that worst-case scenario is occurring or inevitable?

_____
_____
_____
_____
_____
_____
_____
_____
_____
_____

5. **Break into Act 3:** What is the protagonist's new plan to achieve their story goal? Or, based on what they've learned and experienced, perhaps the protagonist has a new goal to achieve in Act 3. If so, what is it and why?

_____
_____
_____
_____
_____
_____
_____
_____

6. **Climax:** What must happen for the protagonist to answer the Central Dramatic Question? What would an ultimate, final confrontation between the protagonist and antagonist look like?

_____
_____
_____
_____
_____
_____
_____
_____

5. CREATING THE SCREENPLAY'S FRAMEWORK

Celebrate! You've built the foundation and framework for your story!

Finished? Take another moment to celebrate! (Seriously, writing a screenplay can be a long process… make sure to bask in the little wins.)

Ready to move on? *Yeah* you are!

SECTION 6

Expanding the Cast of Characters to Work With the Main Character

How Do Supporting Characters Create Change?

Four Common Ways Supporting Characters Challenge Protagonists

Challenge #1: A New Worldview

Challenge #2: Faith in Self

Challenge #3: Cautionary Tale

Challenge #4: Aspirational Model

Supporting Character Brainstorm

Expanding the Cast of Characters to Work With the Main Character

As we talked about earlier, stories – including the movies we love most – tend to involve a transformation of some sort.

Change (transformation) occurs through conflict. We're creatures of habit, after all. People really only change when they're forced to, when it becomes more painful to stay the same than to try something new or different.

To create conflict – e.g. the conditions for change – in our stories, we usually need other characters. Even in a Man. vs. Himself story or a Man vs. Nature story, supporting characters may be needed to add variety and to create enough conflict for the story to sustain an entire movie.

Supporting characters are all about the conflict they bring to the table.

How Do Supporting Characters Create Change?

Of course, you don't want every character in your screenplay to be *physically* at odds with your protagonist.

It takes only a quick glance at your favorite movies to see that often the supporting characters challenge something *within* the main character. That challenge to the main character's worldview, attitude, or beliefs then (if strong enough) causes an effect on the main character's actions. How the challenge affects (changes) the main character reveals new facets and, potentially, growth (transformation).

Change manifests externally but it starts internally.

Four Common Ways Supporting Characters Challenge Protagonists

Challenge #1: A New Worldview

Even people who share a common goal can have different approaches to achieving it. And an individual approach is informed by a person's worldview. People act in line with how they believe the world works.

In this type of challenge, through the conflict created between opposing worldviews on the way to achieving a mutual goal, the protagonist comes to accept a change in his or her worldview.

Hell or High Water is a good example in this category. At the start of the movie, brothers Tanner and Toby have opposite worldviews. Tanner believes in fighting back, even when it's not in your best interest. Toby believes in living with the hand you're dealt.

Over time, Tanner's influence helps Toby to see that in a fight for survival, one lives and the other must die. By the end of the movie Toby accepts that the only way of having a chance at survival is to be willing to fight to the death.

Challenge #2: Faith in Self

Sometimes the change a character needs is to believe in his or her own abilities. But, as noted above, people don't like change. It's uncomfortable. It's scary. If we can avoid it, we will. We only change when we can't get what we want without it.

So even if a character knows a change will benefit them, resistance is still likely. In that case, a supporting character can be a key component in facilitating that transformation.

The Silence of the Lambs is a great example. Hannibal Lecter is anything but a warm-and-fuzzy cheerleader type of mentor to Clarice. But through their relationship he challenges her secret fear that she's not enough, that she's fundamentally inadequate and won't be able to save the victim.

Lecter guides Clarice in solving the puzzle (Who is Buffalo Bill?) – but he doesn't do it for her. He doesn't give her the answers, even though he has them. This conflict (she wants him to give her the answers, he challenges her to figure them out) is what helps her change (and see that she is indeed capable).

Clarice is often frustrated by Lecter, but ultimately she has him to thank for the knowledge and tools she uses to solve the mystery on her own.

Challenge #3: Cautionary Tale

Sometimes we have to see exactly what we don't want, in order to realize (and then go after) what we do want. Just existing as a cautionary tale may not offer much conflict. But when you see this type of supporting character, often their display of what not to do interacts with the main character's pursuit of the goal and causes conflict that way.

6. EXPANDING THE CAST OF CHARACTERS

For example, in *Jaws* we see early conflict from supporting character Mayor Vaughn. After the initial shark attack, Mayor Vaughn refuses to acknowledge the danger. He interferes with Sheriff Brody's efforts to protect the residents.

As a result, the shark claims more victims. The message? This is what happens when good men do nothing. The Mayor's undesirable behavior shows Brody what kind of man he wants to be – one who takes responsibility, who takes action, who fulfills his duty.

As the story continues, Brody sees just how difficult and treacherous a road it is to live that change. But the alternative is failing the people who trust you to lead and protect them. His ideals of staying safe and avoiding conflict are sufficiently challenged, and his new understanding creates a different external action.

Another great example in this category is Ed, the best friend character in *Shaun of the Dead*. Ed shows Shaun what Shaun's future holds if he fails to make the transformation the story is asking of him.

Challenge #4: Aspirational Model

The aspirational model might feel similar in some ways to a "mentor"-type character that would fall into category #2. But there are key differences in how these two types function.

The aspirational model is someone who has what the main character wants. Whether they're aware of it or not, the aspirational model sets the bar for the main character.

And that's how they cause conflict: the high bar or distant finish line they set by example doesn't allow the main character to settle or to take the easy way out. Further, the aspirational model often calls the main character out on his nonsense when the protagonist makes excuses for falling short or wants to give up.

A character in category #2 forces the main character to grow faith in their own abilities. An aspirational model character may not even know they're influencing the main character, but their influence serves to propel the main character forward by showing them what they want and could have. In effect, it's the opposite of a cautionary tale.

An example in this category is Rod Tidwell in *Jerry Maguire*. His marriage sets the bar for Jerry. Over the course of the movie, Jerry's relationship with Dorothy evolves from convenient to real, largely with Rod's example as the ideal Jerry's striving for (whether he'd admit it or not). Rod even calls Jerry out when Jerry tries to fake it and resist the full transformation.

Supporting Character Brainstorm

You may have noticed in each of these examples the supporting character is directly connected to the theme of the movie. In every case, in one way or another, they're helping the protagonist make the change that illustrates the theme.

So when you're looking at your own story, start there to find the purpose of the supporting characters.

What's the theme or the lesson the main character needs to embrace?

_____

_____

_____

_____

_____

With the theme in mind as you work through each of the four categories, think about how other characters could challenge the protagonist to reach that transformed state.

6. EXPANDING THE CAST OF CHARACTERS

1. Brainstorm which supporting characters could possess a "new worldview" for the protagonist to learn from, what the new worldview is, and how the characters will interact.

Character	New Worldview	Interaction
Example: *Love interest*	*One should fight back on principle, even if it causes more harm than necessary.*	*They'll meet in the office and she will introduce him to the underground fight club scene, then they'll develop a romantic relationship but he's more into it than she is.*

2. Which character(s) could force the protagonist to gain faith or confidence in their own ability, and how would they do it?

Character	Specific Quality or Skill	Interaction
Example: Boxing coach	Trust in his unique fighting style, instead of trying to fight in the accepted mainstream style.	Coach will trick him into seeing the value of his unique style through smaller, seemingly unrelated tasks.

6. EXPANDING THE CAST OF CHARACTERS

3. Which character(s) could show the protagonist examples of what he doesn't want to be or do, or of an undesirable outcome that could occur?

Character	Caution	Interaction
Example: *Older brother*	*If you don't fight for what you want, you're guaranteed not to get it and will still sustain "injury".*	*Brother lives at home and seems like a brooding underachiever, but protag will learn he once had a big dream he was too afraid to go the distance for. His anger is now directed at himself and it causes his self-destruction.*

4. Which character(s) could show the protagonist examples of what he does want to be or do, or otherwise set the bar that the protagonist strives to meet?

Character	Aspiration	Interaction
Example: Rival	The kind of person who isn't afraid to enter into a fight, no matter how it might hurt or turn out.	They'll meet in the underground fight club and protag will both admire the rival and also envy him. Protag will strive to be like him and learn from him and they'll develop a real friendship, and ultimately will have to fight.

6. EXPANDING THE CAST OF CHARACTERS

Looking back over your brainstorm, do any of the supporting characters jump out as fitting well into the story and its exploration of the theme? Circle those!

Make any other notes that have come to mind about the supporting characters you'll move forward with in your first draft here:

_____
_____
_____
_____
_____
_____
_____
_____
_____
_____
_____
_____
_____
_____
_____
_____
_____
_____
_____
_____

SECTION 7

Putting It All Together in the Screenplay Outline

What Is a Screenplay Outline?

First, process

Next, format

What goes into an outline?

Simple Story Chart

A basic story arc template

Simple story chart example

Your simple story chart

Notecards

What goes on each card?

What's the difference between a plot point and a beat and a scene?

Tips for getting started with notecards

Does the Break into Act 2 go at the end of Act 1 or the beginning of Act 2?

Notecarding your story

Sequences and Springboards

Why use sequences in your screenplay?

How do Sequences & Springboards work?

What goes in a sequence?

Sequences & Springboards example

Your Sequences & Springboards

Sequence prompts

Incorporating character arc, relationship arcs, subplots

Diagram your story

Your Screenplay Outline

Screenplay Outline Example – *A Quiet Place*

Sequences & Springboards

Breaking down sequences into beat ideas

Expanding the beat list

Beat/scene list screenplay outline

Full scene-by-scene outline excerpt

Putting It All Together in the Screenplay Outline

We've arrived at our last section! Another moment of celebration right now is well deserved.

It's *almost* time to write your script pages. So far you've evaluated and chosen a strong story idea, crafted a sturdy foundation for it, figured out the natural shape of the story and built out a framework using three-act structure and major plot points. And, not to be overlooked, you've also developed a cast of characters centered around and orchestrated to challenge – both internally and externally – your compelling protagonist as they navigate the events of this story.

With all of those vital components thought through, the final pre-writing step we'll cover is putting it all together into an outline that can serve as a map as you write the first draft of your screenplay.

On the way to completing that outline, I'll cover a few of my favorite methods for continuing to discover and flesh out more of your story. Because even with everything you now know, going straight into writing an outline can still feel like a big leap.

In keeping with the rest of this workbook, I want to offer a process that feels manageable. So in the next few sections we'll break down the big task of crafting a screenplay outline into several smaller steps.

What Is a Screenplay Outline?

Let's talk about exactly what you're aiming for when you set out to outline your screenplay. (And whether you even need to write an outline at all.)

As I mentioned early on, every writer is different and you'll want to find the process that works best for *you*. And finding your own best process requires trying out different options.

Although most screenwriters do some form of pre-writing, not everyone puts it down on paper in an outline format. In addition to that, what one writer considers an "outline" might look completely different for another writer's version.

This part of the pre-writing territory is understandably confusing, so let's clarify a few things as best we can.

First, process

By now you've thoughtfully chosen the ingredients that make up your screenplay. You may feel like you have a pretty good sense of the overall shape of the story. So you're wondering if you even need to spend time on an outline right now.

Some writers may choose to forgo more plotting and planning for the moment and dive right into an exploratory first draft. If that option feels right to you, I'd suggest reviewing what you've figured out so far about your story and characters, and then approaching your first draft using the Major Plot Points as milestones. Think of them as targets to aim for as you go. They'll keep your story on track as you fill in the spaces between.

Or, if you feel more comfortable having the plot and scenes figured out in greater detail before writing in screenplay format (doing the creative heavy lifting now rather than while you're writing scenes), the next few sections will walk you through different methods to continue to build out your story.

Which way is better? I truly believe the best way is the one that makes writing as fun and painless as possible for you. Writing a screenplay is a long process (more often a marathon than a sprint), so find ways to make it something you *want* to do.

No matter which strategy you use, you'll end up doing about the same amount of work. The difference is where in the process you spend most of your time. If you find you like planning and doing the heavy lifting up front, that's great! Plot and plan to your heart's content before diving into pages. If you find you like to do minimal planning and work it all out as you write (and rewrite), that works too! It's your choice.

Next, format

One of the questions I'm asked most frequently is, "What should an outline look like?" And the short answer is: it depends on who you ask.

Some writers think of an outline as a summary of the story written in prose form. However, most screenwriters would consider this type of document either a synopsis (if it's short) or a treatment (if it's longer and more detailed). Either way, writing this type of story summary can absolutely be a useful step in your pre-writing process, even if it's not something we'll cover in this workbook.

Some writers think of an outline as a bullet-point list of plot events. For example, screenwriter John August has said in his Script Notes podcast:

> "So I think of an outline as being a document that I'm writing for myself mostly. And it's essentially a plan. It's like a roadmap for sort of how I'm going to get through this script and sort of what the beats are. And so it's really written for my own purpos-

es. It tends to be very short. It can sometimes have little just bullet points for what the things are. And it's basically so I remember what sequence of events happens to get me through this script."

Other writers might call this style of document a "beat sheet," which is a form of outline. A beat sheet is basically a list of the important plot points (or plot "beats") in a story. You might think of it as a list of the significant moments, actions, or reversals that will occur in the screenplay.

For our purposes, an outline is similar to a beat sheet, but includes a more detailed description of the story beats or individual scenes.

Again on the Script Notes podcast, John August and his co-host Craig Mazin have described outlines thusly:

> John: "An outline is, to me, a much more – a better fleshed out version of the beat sheet that actually shows – tends to show scene by scene, definitely sequence by sequence how you're getting from point A to point B, what is introduced where, the callbacks to things. It's a longer document."

> Craig: "I mean, an outline is basically a very thorough beat sheet, where you're not just saying things like 'police station, they interrogate the suspect.' An outline would say 'Police station. This person and this person interrogate the suspect. They want to know this. She says this. They're not sure. They decide to go talk to somebody else. Next bit.'"

What goes into an outline?

In this section we'll begin to build an outline document. If it's not clear by now, you should do so in a way that makes sense to you and that will be useful as you write your draft. That will be a little (or a lot) different for everyone. But there's no point in writing a document that doesn't help you along the way. The point of writing an outline isn't to have written an outline – it's to move you toward a finished screenplay.

So what goes into the outline should be useful in writing your screenplay pages. Your outline will contain plot events, character actions and reactions, reveals, reversals, etc. It's the stuff you're going to write in your screenplay. In other words, your outline will be made up of the moments needed to tell the story you want to tell.

Now, how do you come up with those moments? While some screenwriters may simply work it all out directly in a beat sheet or outline document, there are other ways to continue to develop your story, to plan the screenplay more and more granularly before you formalize it in an outline.

The next sections are meant to give you options to do so. Experiment, try different strategies and tools, and find your own best process as you go.

Simple Story Chart

One quick way to take what you already know about your story and connect the narrative dots is with this simple story chart. This is still a fairly high-level view of the story, but it offers a sense of how the story flows from beginning to end and whether the parts you've put together are effectively creating the big picture you're going for.

As we touched on before, nothing in a story happens in a vacuum. The parts of a story all relate to each other, and you can use what you know about one element to "do the story math" and figure out others.

The Inciting Incident relates to the Break into Act 2. The character setup relates to the thematic lightbulb moment near the end of Act 2. The Break into Act 2 relates to the Climax, etc.

When you understand how the math of a story works, you understand the how and why – the function of each part of the equation. And that understanding makes it easier to create an effective story.

And there are a lot of ways we can check the math of your story before you even have it fully outlined. Including the simple story chart in this section that you might find useful as you're working out your story and double-checking the math to make sure it all holds together.

A basic story arc template

You know a story essentially boils down to "someone wants something badly and goes after it against strong opposition."

If we told that story in very simple terms and broad strokes, it would go something like this:

- This type of person...
- Is suddenly confronted with this problem (or opportunity)...
- And must deal with it or else...
- So they decide to... even though they're up against...
- And they pursue that goal actively and consistently despite ongoing and escalating opposition.
- What they experience also challenges something within the character...
- Until it becomes impossible to ignore the realization...

7. PUTTING IT ALL TOGETHER

- And the character re-commits to their goal...
- Employing new strategies and informed by their new knowledge, until they achieve resolution.

Here it is in a chart showing where in the screenplay each part occurs:

First part of Act 1	This type of person...
Inciting Incident	Is suddenly confronted with this problem (or opportunity)...
The rest of Act 1	And must deal with it or else...
Break into Act 2	So they decide to... even though they're up against...
Act 2 (plot)	And they pursue that goal actively and consistently despite ongoing and escalating opposition...
Simultaneously in Act 2 (character arc)	What they experience also challenges something within the character...
End of Act 2 or sometimes beginning of Act 3	Until it becomes impossible to ignore the realization...
Break into Act 3	And the character re-commits to their goal... (or wants something new, depending on what they've learned)
Act 3	Employing new strategies and informed by their new knowledge, until they achieve resolution.

THE SCREENPLAY OUTLINE WORKBOOK

As I say with so many screenwriting tips, don't dismiss this chart just because it seems simple. These "obvious" things are essential to your story yet they are often overlooked. And if these things aren't in place, you're building your screenplay on a weak or faulty foundation.

Simple story chart example

Let's use *Bridesmaids* as an example. If we lay out the basic story in our chart, it would look something like this:

First part of Act 1	A woman who's stuck and hiding her dissatisfaction with her life… (*this is the starting point of the protagonist's arc*)
Inciting Incident	Is asked to be the Maid of Honor for her best friend… (*a problem or opportunity is introduced*)
The rest of Act 1	And she wants to do it to maintain her friendship, which is the only good thing left in her life… (*this is what's at stake in the story*)
Break into Act 2	So she commits to fulfilling her Maid of Honor duties even though it means she has to wrangle a motley group of bridesmaids, and is up against Perfect Helen who wants to steal away her best friend… (*the protagonist's solution to the problem, but it won't be easy!*)
Act 2 (plot)	She actively and consistently struggles to organize bridal activities and we see Perfect Helen taking action to sabotage her and steal away the best friend. (*actively pursuing the goal*)
Simultaneously in Act 2 (character arc)	Seeing where the other women are in their lives also forces her to confront why she's stuck and dissatisfied with her own life and what she really wants… (*and being changed by the experience*)

7. PUTTING IT ALL TOGETHER

End of Act 2 or sometimes beginning of Act 3	Until she finally realizes she's responsible for her own happiness, and if she wants to get unstuck she has to go for what she wants. (*this is the thematic lesson, the crux of the character's transformation*)
Break into Act 3	She starts trying to right the wrongs she's made and get the life she wants... (*new action informed by what she's experienced and learned*)
Act 3	And soon gets an opportunity to help her best friend, proving she's grown and has a new outlook, and reclaims her spot as Maid of Honor. (*and demonstrating the transformation*)

This is a quick and simple way to plan out your story in big chunks and important turning points. And you can see how the parts that should relate to each other, do. The story holds together. There's a certain dramatic logic to it.

Can we get more granular with the story? Add in more major plot points, break down Act 2 into smaller, more manageable-to-write chunks? Definitely. And we will, very soon. But this chart is a good place to start as it gives you a way to look at the story as a whole. To check whether all of the pieces are in place for a satisfying story, before you put more work into creating each part and detail.

A script might have all the "right" plot points in all the "right" places, but if the parts of the story don't relate to each other to create meaning, the script will feel empty. It won't move us. In a good story, the sum is greater than the parts.

Your simple story chart:

Try filling in the simple story chart for your story:

First part of Act 1	This type of person...
Inciting Incident	Is suddenly confronted with this problem (or opportunity)...
The rest of Act 1	And must deal with it or else...
Break into Act 2	So they decides to... even though they're up against...

Act 2 (plot)	And then pursues that goal actively and consistently despite ongoing and escalating opposition...
Simultaneously in Act 2 (character arc)	What they experience also challenges something within the character...
End of Act 2 or sometimes beginning of Act 3	Until it becomes impossible to ignore the realization...
Break into Act 3	And the character re-commits to their goal... (or wants something new, depending on what they've learned)
Act 3	Employing new strategies and informed by their new knowledge, until they achieve resolution.

Notecards

When you have a good feel for the high-level shape and flow of your story, the next exercise you may want to try is laying your story out in more detail using notecards.

Notecards are great if you want a tactile activity while you're plotting out your story. Switching it up (and stepping away from your computer) can help spur your brain into action.

If you're familiar with *Save the Cat!*, you may already know all about "The Board," although writers have been using some version of notecards, corkboard, sticky notes, whiteboard, etc. to break stories since before STC – probably since the advent of the technology. If you don't have a corkboard available, you can arrange your cards on a big table or even the floor (which I actually prefer – it's easier to re-order them when they're not tacked to a board).

Perhaps the most popular way to arrange the notecards is in four horizontal rows:

- Row 1 represents Act 1.
- Row 2 represents the first half of Act 2, or what many people call Act 2A.
- Row 3 represents the second half of Act 2, or Act 2B.
- Row 4 represents Act 3.

This arrangement divides your story into four equal portions. If you refer back to the 3 Act Overview section, you'll see it corresponds to the proportions we talked about there.

What goes on each card?

As with so many process-related questions, there isn't one "right" way to use notecards. Some writers fill up their notecards with detailed descriptions, or brain dump all of their ideas in a catch-all system. Others limit themselves, maybe a handful of words, or one sentence per card. Some writers create one notecard per scene. Others follow a method popularized by *Save the Cat!*, creating one notecard for each of a movie's "40 major story beats," as author Blake Snyder proposed. And anywhere in between!

The idea is to use the notecards to work through and lay out your story in its entirety, in whatever way makes the most sense to you.

7. PUTTING IT ALL TOGETHER

What's the difference between a plot point and a beat and a scene?

You might be confused about how many cards you should end up with on your board, and that's understandable. The answer is that it depends on what you're putting on each card. Is it a beat, a plot point, a scene, or something else entirely?

If you follow the *Save the Cat!* notecarding/board method, you're meant to end up with 40 cards, each one representing a major "story beat." If you assign one card for each scene, you'll end up with more than 40 – probably many more. The exact number depends on the pacing and length of your story, and how you view what makes a scene.

For our purposes, a beat is a building block – a significant piece of the story. It's an important plot event, character action, turning point, or dramatic or comedic moment.

A scene, on the other hand, is generally defined as a unit of dramatic action that takes place in one location. And if this feels confusing, that's understandable – there's definite overlap there.

To throw yet one more thing into the mix: what about plot points? The plot is the sequence of events in your story, in which we generally track a character's pursuit of a goal. A plot point is an event that changes the character's orientation to that objective. In other words, a plot point is a story event that moves the protagonist either closer to or farther from the story goal.

A beat may be made up of several scenes. A beat may be made up of several plot points. A plot point may play out over several scenes. One scene could conceivably contain more than one plot point.

And yes, it *is* confusing. But, honestly? Most people use the terms pretty interchangeably unless they're being very technical about it. So try not to get too bogged down in semantics. Think in terms of what you can see happening on screen. Write it piece by piece on your notecards in the way that makes sense to you.

Tips for getting started with notecards

Whether you're going to card 40 story beats or every scene, a good place to start is with your Major Plot Points. Those important story turns, which work together to define the overall shape, will show up in almost any summary or description of your story – they're that important.

So, write those on notecards and place them where they should fall in the timeline of your movie:

- ◇ The Inciting Incident will land at or just before the middle of Row 1.
- ◇ The Break into Act 2 will land at the end of Row 1 or the start of Row 2 (your choice*).
- ◇ The Midpoint will land at the end of Row 2 or the start of Row 3 (your choice*).
- ◇ The Low Point will land somewhere toward the end of Row 3 (and may play out over more than one notecard).
- ◇ The Break into Act 3 will land at the end of Row 3 or the start of Row 4 (your choice*).
- ◇ The Climax will almost definitely play out over more than one notecard and will land in the latter part of Row 4.

> **Does the Break into Act 2 go at the end of Act 1 or the beginning of Act 2?**
>
> Personally, I think of this and other pivotal story events as a hinge that connects two parts of the script. I'll often place it at the end of the first row initially, but it may move to the start of the next row as I figure out the scenes with more specificity. It depends on what the particular plot events are that we're dealing with. In some scripts the event that serves as the Break into Act 2 feels like it goes at the end of Act 1, in others it feels like it goes at the start of Act 2. Put it where it feels right to you for the story you're working on.

Next comes a fun, messy, frustrating, exciting process of filling in the story gaps between your Major Plot Points.

How do you approach it? Start wherever you like, and start filling in what you know happens in the story. Write down every beat, plot point, or scene you can think of, and slot them in where they likely go in Act 1, Act 2A, Act 2B, or Act 3.

Draw from the other planning and prep work you've done, including the Simple Story Chart, the protagonist's introduction, etc. Generate cards by noting down what happens in the various parts of the story you've already thought through:

Think about character arc, and what we need to see in order to understand how the character is at the beginning of the story (needs the change), the transformation he experiences along the way (learns the lesson), and how he can demonstrate or prove he's accepted the lesson in the end (embraces the change).

Think about supporting characters and their relationships with the protagonist. Think about the antagonist's actions. Add the new notecards where you think they might go.

When the board seems fairly full, read through what you have and see how it flows. You'll find gaps to fill – go for it! You'll find cards that are definitely in the wrong spot – move them or set them aside to come back to later.

Keep going over the story, smoothing and finessing so that it all flows from one notecard to the next until your whole story is there in front of you.

Notecarding your story

If you're ready to try this out, grab a pack of 3x5 or 4x6 notecards and get started! If you don't have the room to lay them all out in one spot, there's one other trick I'd recommend: use sticky notes instead of notecards.

The medium-sized, 3"x3" square sticky notes can be used on a wall, door, or window pretty easily. If you keep it brief, the smallest, 1.5"x 2" notes can be used in a file folder (or even the print version of this workbook!) for a portable version of your board.

Sequences and Springboards

And one last method we'll cover for fleshing out your story is Sequences & Springboards. It might be helpful to note that you can try Sequences & Springboards before notecarding or after, do one or both, or none at all. These methods are offered as options for you to use to discover your story and plan what you're going to write in your screenplay; they are not requirements in and of themselves.

You may have heard of the sequence structure method, or the idea that movies can be broken down into a series of sequences that make up the story as a whole. The common template is eight sequences, which is two sequences per quarter of the screenplay.

Not every movie fits this pattern, of course, but when we're in the process of creating a story, sequences can be a useful tool. Begin here, but hold it loosely. Be willing to adjust as you discover more about your story.

Why use sequences in your screenplay?

It's pretty easy to see how sequences work in the big picture. They break the larger whole into a series of eight smaller steps.

```
| ACT 1                 | ACT 2                                      | ACT 3             |
| Seq. 1 | Seq. 2       | Seq. 3 | Seq. 4 | Seq. 5 | Seq. 6       | Seq. 7 | Seq. 8   |
```

Thinking in eight sequences gives you a little more guidance in shaping and structuring your story. It can be a good intermediary step on your way to a complete outline and writing your screenplay draft. Sequences can help ensure there's a nice progression in your plot, and create a sense of momentum.

Full disclosure: I like this method so much that I teach it in both my "Idea to Outline" and "Finish Your Screenplay" classes.

How do Sequences & Springboards work?

With this method we look at each quarter of the screenplay as made up of two sequences. Each sequence ends in a springboard event, which launches the next sequence. (Except the final sequence, after which the movie is over.)

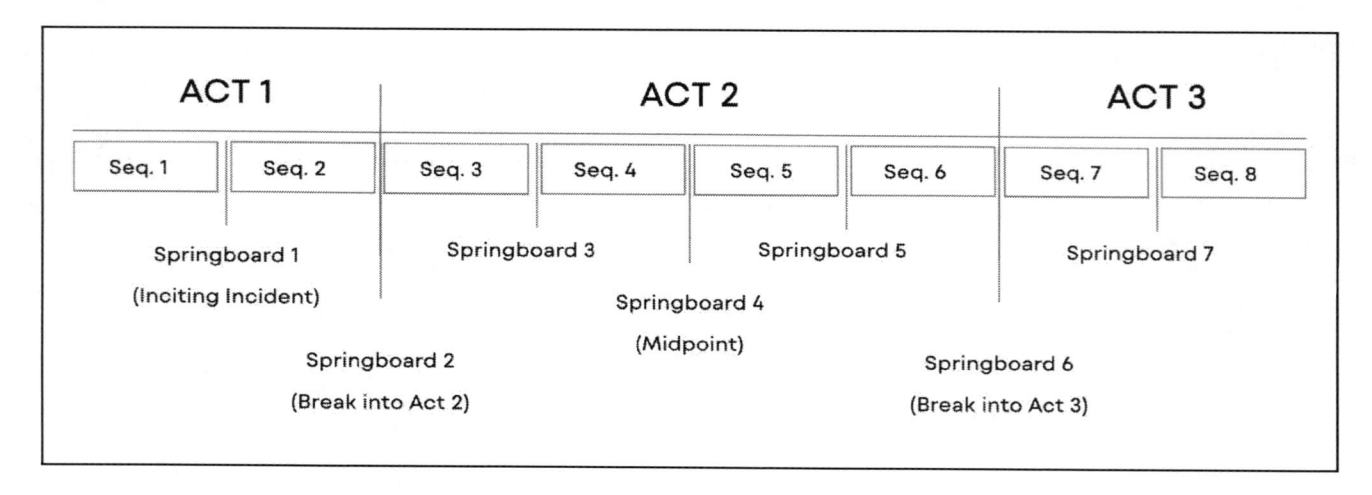

```
| ACT 1                 | ACT 2                                      | ACT 3             |
| Seq. 1 | Seq. 2       | Seq. 3 | Seq. 4 | Seq. 5 | Seq. 6       | Seq. 7 | Seq. 8   |

Springboard 1              Springboard 3            Springboard 5          Springboard 7
(Inciting Incident)
                                          Springboard 4
                                          (Midpoint)
        Springboard 2                                      Springboard 6
        (Break into Act 2)                                 (Break into Act 3)
```

You can see that some of the springboards are plot points you've already figured out. You can fill in those blanks quite easily and then use them to help you figure out other parts of the story.

The sequences in between the springboards form a bridge. The bridge, or sequence, is all of the events that take us from one springboard to the next. In the case of Sequence 1, you'll want to think about where your character is when the story begins. It's the "normal world" that will be interrupted by the Inciting Incident. Think of Sequence 1 as providing

7. PUTTING IT ALL TOGETHER

the context we need to understand how and why the Inciting Incident creates a problem that the protagonist must act on.

What goes in a sequence?

In many ways a sequence tells its own mini-story, so it should have all the elements you know any story needs.

There's a beginning, middle, and end, aka the setup, escalation, resolution. There's a line of action created by someone pursuing something. There's opposition and obstacles.

And ideally you want your audience to get and stay invested so they don't check out partway through. You want your audience to care. That means you have to let them know what they're rooting for and give them enough information so they want to root for it.

Unlike a complete story (like a whole screenplay), a sequence benefits from the context created by other sequences that have come before. You're building on what you've already established rather than starting from scratch. So in each sequence you may not need to establish anew what's at stake. But you'll likely want to remind the audience of the overall story stakes or escalate the stakes in some way, so the story maintains a certain degree of urgency.

Sequences & Springboards example

If you were writing a movie like *The Ring*, your Sequences & Springboards could look something like this:

ACT 1:

Sequence 1: Single mom Rachel, an investigative journalist, and her young son, Aidan, try to cope with the sudden and mysterious death of Aidan's teenage cousin, Katie.

> **Inciting Incident / Springboard 1:** Katie's mom implores Rachel to investigate Katie's death, tapping into Rachel's feelings of guilt and inadequacy.

Sequence 2: Rachel learns of several more related deaths, and — though skeptical — tracks down a "cursed" videotape that is rumored to be the cause.

> **Break into Act 2 / Springboard 2:** Rachel watches the tape. She receives a phone call, warning her that she has seven days to live.

ACT 2A:

Sequence 3: Rachel attempts to find if and how the tape could possibly be a real threat.

> **Springboard 3:** Rachel visits the lone survivor from Katie's group of friends, Becca, and finds her nearly comatose in a mental institution. But Becca flips out at the sight of a TV. She finally speaks: "Four days." Shaken, Rachel is now convinced the curse is real.

Sequence 4: Rachel races against time to research the images on the tape in order to track its origin. The tape begins to break through to torment Rachel's real world.

> **Midpoint / Springboard 4:** Aidan watches the videotape, and now he's cursed too! After this, Rachel has to solve the mystery in order to save not only herself, but also her son.

ACT 2B:

Sequence 5: Rachel follows the clues on the tape to the Morgan family, and learns they had a daughter.

> **Springboard 5:** Rachel discovers the picture that Aidan drew for her is of the Morgans' house — a place he's never seen. When asked, Aidan reveals "the girl" told him to draw it.

Sequence 6: Rachel investigates the Morgans' daughter and learns she had "visions" which hurt people. She was kept in an institution where her interview sessions were videotaped. Rachel follows the clues to a remote location.

> **Low Point + Break into Act 3 / Springboard 6:** Rachel's reached a dead end and has run out of time. Her death is imminent. (Low point) But a last minute clue is uncovered. There's one more thing to try… (Break into Act 3)

ACT 3:

Sequence 7: Rachel follows the clues into an underground well, finds the girl's skeleton, and communes with the dead girl to give her closure. Rachel doesn't die.

> **Springboard 7:** Just when Rachel thinks it's all over, Aidan reveals it's not! Rachel realizes her son's life is still in danger.

Climax / Sequence 8: Rachel finds out the real reason the curse didn't kill her — she made a copy of the tape and passed it on. To save her son, she helps him do the same.

As you can see, these are pretty broad descriptions. There are a lot of details I've left out, including an important supporting character! And that's okay at this phase. You're building your story house piece by piece. Focus on the main character at first.

Your Sequences & Springboards

As with the other methods, there isn't one way you have to approach this. A good starting point is to fill in the Major Plot Points for their corresponding springboards. Then take each sequence-level section of story, and see if you can summarize what's happening there.

Describe how one springboard propels the next section of story, which results in the next springboard. Look to your earlier notes and exercises for events that can serve as the additional springboards – the ones that aren't already filled in as Major Plot Points – and to fill in brief descriptions for the sequences that bridge from one springboard to the next.

At this stage of story planning, we're looking for a simple description of the action that occurs in the 10-15 pages of each sequence. What the character is trying to do, or the mini-goal they're trying to achieve.

Sequence prompts

If you're having trouble coming up with the sequence descriptions for your story, try these prompts to get unstuck:

ACT 1:

Context, it sets up what the protagonist wants to do (the story goal).

Sequence 1: We meet the protagonist, we see their status quo, and we learn who they are through their defining characteristic. Their behavior also shows us the starting point of their character arc – the "before" picture of their transformation – and how they need the lesson or change this journey will teach them.

> **Inciting Incident / Springboard 1:** Introduces a problem (or opportunity) the protagonist must contend with. You can also think of this as "why the story starts now."

Sequence 2: The character comes up with their best or only "solution" to the problem/opportunity, and we see why they must embark on this mission or journey, even though it's a big, audacious, dangerous thing to do. We may see: why they should do it, what happens if they don't, what happens if they fail, what they're risking in order to go after it, etc. You're getting the audience to root for the character to do what they're about to do.

> **Break into Act 2 / Springboard 2:** The main conflict is clear and the protagonist has a story goal or plan of action to pursue.

ACT 2:

Conflict and escalation, it shows the protagonist pursuing their goal and encountering opposition and obstacles, and being changed/transformed by the experience of it.

~ In each of the next four sequences, think about where the conflict is coming from, how the main conflict progresses, and what happens in the character arc because of the main conflict ~

Sequence 3: The first step or strategy in pursuing the goal. The protagonist may also believe at this point that success is imminent or the path they're on will be easy, but they are wrong. You can also think about the "promise of the premise," a.k.a. making sure to exploit the entertainment hooks of your story here.

> **Springboard 3:** A plot event (usually smaller than the Major Plot Points) that launches and/or causes the next sequence.

Sequence 4: The next step or strategy in pursuing the goal. They may need a new strategy because the first one didn't work out, or they may simply be doing what naturally or logically comes next in a process.

> **Midpoint / Springboard 4:** Raises the stakes and/or increases the opposition to achieving the story goal, and as a result injects new energy into the story, gets us to keep leaning in, and sometimes drastically changes the direction the story's headed.

Sequence 5: The effects of the midpoint play out. The character is still trying to move toward achieving their goal and still trying (but probably struggling) to hold onto their old, "flawed" way of doing things. There may be some regrouping, adjusting, or gathering new resources and allies, and the protagonist may feel like he's struggling to keep up in some way, even if he's also seemingly getting closer to success.

> **Springboard 5:** A plot event (usually smaller than the Major Plot Points) that launches and/or causes the next sequence.

Sequence 6: The character continues to pursue their goal, although it may seem impossible by now. This sequence usually culminates in a "low point" for the protagonist where

7. PUTTING IT ALL TOGETHER

they feel on the verge of failure, or that they'll never be able to achieve the story goal, or they may realize they've been pursuing the wrong thing all along. Often they'll have a "lightbulb moment" or pep talk of some sort, where the protagonist faces the lesson of the story's theme. They're probably not ready to fully embrace it yet, but may recognize for the first time what the lesson is.

> **Break into Act 3 / Springboard 6:** Usually characterized by a new plan to achieve the goal, or a new goal altogether. This will be informed by what the character has learned over the course of Act 2.

ACT 3:

Resolution, it shows the protagonist confronting and resolving the main conflict. They achieve the goal or not, and we get an answer to the Central Dramatic Question.

Sequence 7: This sequence is often either preparing for the final battle, or going into what the protagonist thinks is the final battle, only to learn they were wrong and there's a different final battle to engage in before it's all over.

> **Springboard 7:** A plot event that launches us into the final, climactic sequence of the movie.

Sequence 8: Where the "final battle" or climactic confrontation with the antagonist plays out. This is the protagonist's last chance to achieve the goal, determine the outcome of the main conflict, and prove or demonstrate their transformation. After the final battle, we usually see a bit of wrap-up to give closure.

Use the blank worksheets here to brainstorm Sequences & Springboards for your story:

THE SCREENPLAY OUTLINE WORKBOOK

Project title: _____

ACT 1:

⋄ Sequence 1: _____

_____
_____
_____
_____
_____

  ○ Inciting Incident / SB 1: _____

_____
_____
_____
_____
_____

⋄ Sequence 2: _____

_____
_____
_____
_____

  ○ Break into Act 2 / SB 2: _____

_____
_____
_____
_____
_____

7. PUTTING IT ALL TOGETHER

ACT 2A:

- ⬦ Sequence 3: _____
_____
_____
_____
_____

  - ○ Springboard 3: _____
  _____
  _____
  _____
  _____
  _____

- ⬦ Sequence 4: _____
_____
_____
_____
_____

  - ○ Midpoint / SB 4: _____
  _____
  _____
  _____
  _____
  _____
  _____

ACT 2B:

- Sequence 5: _____
  _____
  _____
  _____
  _____
  _____

  - Springboard 5: _____
    _____
    _____
    _____
    _____

- Sequence 6: _____
  _____
  _____
  _____
  _____

  - Low Point + Break into Act 3 / SB 6: _____
    _____
    _____
    _____
    _____
    _____
    _____
    _____

7. PUTTING IT ALL TOGETHER

ACT 3:

- ◇ Sequence 7: _____
_____
_____
_____
_____

  - ○ Springboard 7: : _____
  _____
  _____
  _____

- ◇ Sequence 8 / Climax: _____
_____
_____
_____
_____
_____
_____
_____
_____
_____

THE SCREENPLAY OUTLINE WORKBOOK

Project title: _____

ACT 1:

♦ Sequence 1: _____
_____
_____
_____
_____

 o Inciting Incident / SB 1: _____
_____
_____
_____
_____

♦ Sequence 2: _____
_____
_____
_____
_____

 o Break into Act 2 / SB 2: _____
_____
_____
_____
_____

7. PUTTING IT ALL TOGETHER

ACT 2A:

- ◇ Sequence 3: _____
  _____
  _____
  _____
  _____

  - ○ Springboard 3: _____
    _____
    _____
    _____
    _____
    _____

- ◇ Sequence 4: _____
  _____
  _____
  _____
  _____

  - ○ Midpoint / SB 4: _____
    _____
    _____
    _____
    _____
    _____
    _____

ACT 2B:

- ◇ Sequence 5: _____
  _____
  _____
  _____
  _____
  _____

  - ○ Springboard 5: _____
    _____
    _____
    _____
    _____

- ◇ Sequence 6: _____
  _____
  _____
  _____
  _____

  - ○ Low Point + Break into Act 3 / SB 6: _____
    _____
    _____
    _____
    _____
    _____
    _____
    _____

7. PUTTING IT ALL TOGETHER

ACT 3:

- ⬥ Sequence 7: _____
_____
_____
_____
_____

  - ○ Springboard 7: : _____
  _____
  _____
  _____

- ⬥ Sequence 8 / Climax: _____
_____
_____
_____
_____
_____
_____
_____
_____
_____
_____

Incorporating character arc, relationship arcs, subplots

You might look at the example above or even your own sequence list and think — that's not the whole story. There are important characters and plants and payoffs that aren't even mentioned. And you're right — we're not all the way there yet. With each step we're growing the story a little more.

Once you have the basic sequence outline, you can return to your character arc, supporting character and relationship idea brainstorms and find more details to flesh out the story.

With the relationships you've identified, can you brainstorm a list of steps that will demonstrate how they'll play out? Can you weave those into the sequences? They don't have to be set in stone on the first try — just see if you can guess approximately where each beat of the relationship will land. As you break the story down more and more granularly you'll adjust and smooth the flow, just as with the notecard method.

Let's use *Game Night* as an example of how this part of the process might look.

Our sequences and springboards might look like this:

ACT 1

- Sequence 1: Game Night hosts Max and Annie want to have a baby but the stress of Max's rivalry with his brother Brooks is destroying Max's fertility.
    - Inciting Incident / SB 1: Brooks arrives, driving Max's dream car.
- Sequence 2: There's genuine brotherly love there, but Brooks undermines Max in every way.
    - Break into Act 2 / SB 2: Max knows he must finally beat Brooks at game night.

ACT 2A

- Sequence 3: The Game Night crew convenes at Brooks's fancy rented home. Brooks announces he's arranged an epic new game: a staged kidnapping that they'll have to solve. As that gets underway…
    - Springboard 3: Actual kidnappers arrive, brawl with Brooks, and kidnap him.
- Sequence 4: Max, Annie, and friends break into couples and begin to play, pursuing different leads and trying to solve the "case", which they still think is all a game.

- Midpoint / SB 4: The crew learns the kidnapping was real. Max, Annie, and Brooks narrowly escape the kidnappers.

ACT 2B

- Sequence 5: Brooks explains what he's mixed up in, sacrifices himself to the kidnappers and the crew comes up with a new plan to save him.
  - Springboard 5: The crew convinces neighbor Gary, a cop, to have an impromptu game night.
- Sequence 6: They get info from Gary's police computer, infiltrate the house, and steal the needed Faberge egg.
  - Break into Act 3 / SB 6: The crew arrives to the rendezvous just under the wire, but the kidnappers plan to kill them all.

ACT 3

- Sequence 7: Gary arrives to help and a shootout ensues. A twist: he reveals he staged the second kidnapping as part of a game. A double twist: actual bad guys arrive – the ones Brooks was really mixed up with.
  - Springboard 7: The real bad guys take Brooks with plans to kill him.
- Sequence 8: Max and Annie race to the airfield to save Brooks before the bad guys can escape. Months later, everyone's together again for Game Night and Annie is pregnant.

In *Game Night*, there are a lot of relationships (and characters) to track so I'll focus on the one between Max and Annie for our example here. They're dealing with the issue of whether they'll have kids. Knowing this, I might first come up with a list of beats in this story arc:

- Max and Annie are having trouble getting pregnant.
- Max's feelings of inferiority are killing their chances. He needs to beat Brooks to solve this problem.
- Annie gets a first hint that Max is worried about losing the freedom to do what they want if they have a kid.
- Annie realizes the stress wasn't from Brooks, it was from the idea of having a baby.
- Max learns Brooks has been lying because he felt like he couldn't measure up to Max.

- Max tells Annie he wants to have a baby. No longer wants to be like Brooks.
- Annie reveals she's pregnant.

So then you can take your list of sequences and see where the new beats fit in (some are already there, that's okay). In this step, you might also make notes to yourself of things to establish. Later you can then fill in additional scenes from those notes, creating the connective tissue of your story.

This is what my work in progress would look like (with what I've just added in bold):

ACT 1

- Sequence 1: Game Night hosts Max and Annie want to have a baby but the stress of Max's rivalry with his brother Brooks is destroying Max's fertility.

  - **Max and Annie are having trouble getting pregnant.**
  - Inciting Incident / SB 1: Brooks arrives, driving Max's dream car.

- Sequence 2: There's genuine brotherly love there, but Brooks undermines Max in every way.

  - **Max's feelings of inferiority are killing their chances. He needs to beat Brooks. (Make sure to show Max feeling inferior to Brooks in set up.)**
  - Break into Act 2 / SB 2: Max knows he must finally beat Brooks at game night.

ACT 2A

- Sequence 3: The Game Night crew convenes at Brooks's fancy rented home. Brooks announces he's arranged an epic new game: a staged kidnapping that they'll have to solve. As that gets underway…

  - Springboard 3: Actual kidnappers arrive, brawl with Brooks, and kidnap him.

- Sequence 4: Max, Annie, and friends break into couples and begin to play, pursuing different leads and trying to solve the "case", which they still think is all a game.

  - **Annie gets the first hint from Max that he's worried about losing their freedom if they have a kid.**
  - Midpoint / SB 4: The crew learns the kidnapping was real. Max, Annie, and Brooks narrowly escape the kidnappers.

ACT 2B

- Sequence 5: Brooks explains what he's mixed up in, sacrifices himself to the kidnappers and the crew comes up with a new plan to save him.

7. PUTTING IT ALL TOGETHER

- o Springboard 5: The crew convinces neighbor Gary, a cop, to have an impromptu game night.

- ◇ Sequence 6: They get info from Gary's police computer, infiltrate the house, and steal the needed Faberge egg.

  - o **Annie realizes Max's stress wasn't from Brooks, it was from the idea of having a baby.**
  - o Break into Act 3 / SB 6: The crew arrives to the rendezvous just under the wire, but the kidnappers plan to kill them all.

ACT 3

Sequence 7: Gary arrives to help and a shootout ensues. A twist: he reveals he staged the second kidnapping as part of a game. A double twist: actual bad guys arrive — the ones Brooks was really mixed up with.

- o **Max learns Brooks has been lying because he felt like he couldn't measure up to Max. They both thought the grass was greener.**
- o Springboard 7: The real bad guys take Brooks with plans to kill him.

- ◇ Sequence 8: Max and Annie race to the airfield to save Brooks before the bad guys can escape. Months later, everyone's together again for Game Night and Annie is pregnant.

  - o **Max tells Annie he wants to have a baby. No longer wants to be like Brooks.**
  - o **Annie reveals she's pregnant.**

When you feel good about how that relationship arc is playing out, you can move onto the next one. And you can do this for each relationship, subplot, or story thread you want to weave into the story.

Again, at this point this is all rough and subject to change. That's okay — it's a process of discovery and it's almost never linear. Right now we're simply trying to find and organize what we know about the story. Adding details to fill in the characters, relationships, and plot, and growing the story step by step.

Diagram your story

As you may have noticed, when you're working through a new idea and figuring out which puzzle pieces you need to build your screenplay, you end up with a lot of stuff. Almost as if each decision you've made about your story has manifested in a real puzzle piece, and as you've worked your way through the development process they've been left sprinkled behind you like a trail of breadcrumbs.

Even if you've found all of the right elements through your development exercises, leaving those pieces scattered around means you're not able to see all of your story stuff together, to check for connections and alignment. To see if there are any glaring holes or gaps in your thinking.

Having one place to collect all of the pieces and parts that make up your screenplay means that you can start to see it all in context, which allows you to productively write from what you've collected.

That's why I put together the worksheet you'll find on the following pages. Use it at any time in your process that you find helpful, when you want to see your whole story in one place. Mark up the diagram with notes on your protagonist's transformation, the Major Plot Points, and other story elements. Use the space below the diagram to write out the broad strokes of each sequence, map out relationships or subplots, or anything else you find useful. And you can keep your story diagram in front of you while you're writing as a reminder of what the big picture looks like, as well as the parts that make it up – so as not to lose sight of any of the essential pieces along the way.

(You can also use this worksheet to clarify and memorialize your thoughts about a screenplay or movie you're analyzing, too – a great practice while you're learning and solidifying all of the concepts!)

Story & structure worksheet guide

The diagram shown below includes numbers to make it easier to reference and explain the various parts. On the next pages you'll find several blank worksheets for you to use with your own projects, and you can download additional PDF copies on the Write + Co. website – writeandco.com.

7. PUTTING IT ALL TOGETHER

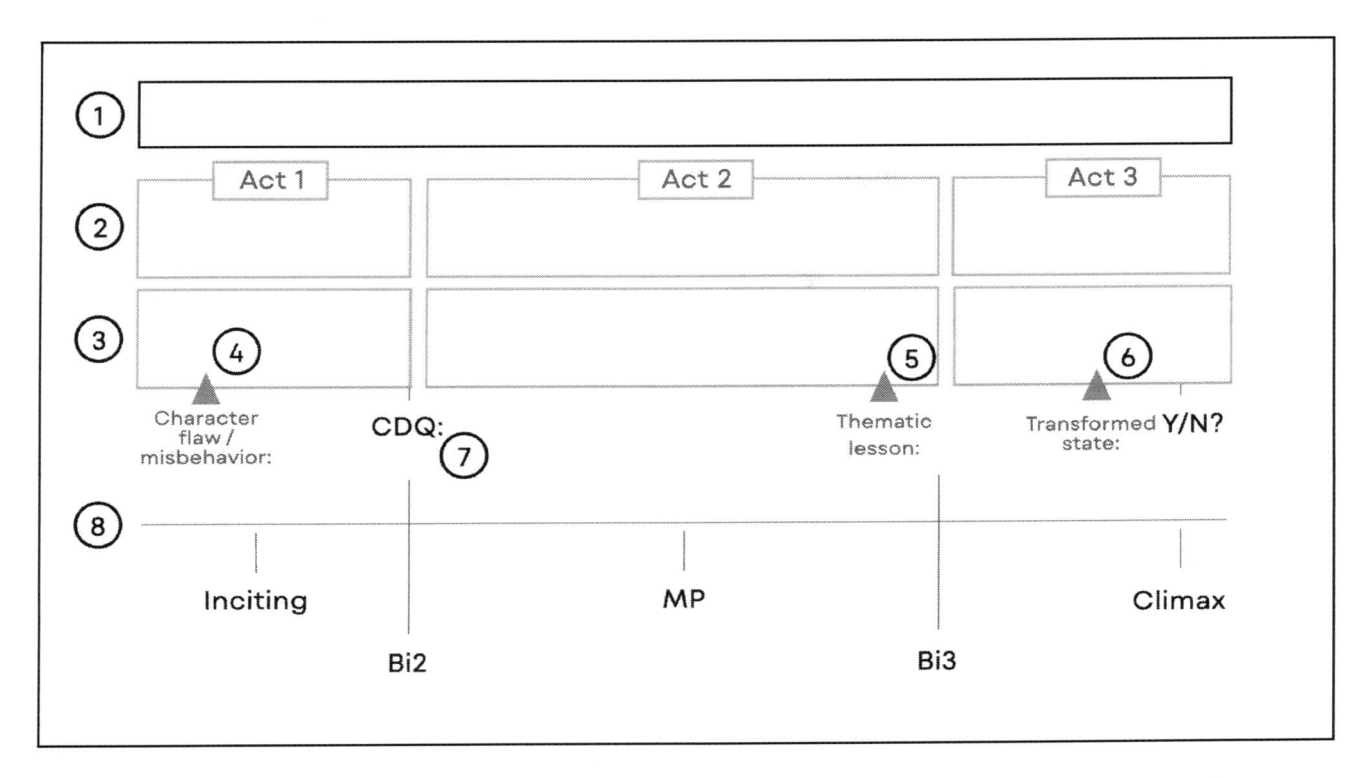

```
┌─────────────────────────────────────────────────────────────┐
│  ①  [                                                    ]  │
│                                                             │
│           Act 1            Act 2              Act 3         │
│  ②  [          ] [                      ] [              ]  │
│                                                             │
│  ③  [    ④     ] [                  ⑤  ] [      ⑥        ]  │
│         ▲                            ▲           ▲          │
│     Character      CDQ:         Thematic   Transformed Y/N? │
│      flaw /             ⑦        lesson:      state:        │
│    misbehavior:                                             │
│                                                             │
│  ⑧     │              │              │              │       │
│     Inciting                  MP                  Climax    │
│              Bi2                      Bi3                   │
└─────────────────────────────────────────────────────────────┘
```

You can probably figure out much of what goes where on your own — and maybe even come up with your own adaptations that you prefer — but to get you started I'll walk you through how I use it.

1.) In the long box at the top, write your simple story concept. (For example: Jaws is about a guy trying to keep his town safe from a killer shark.) This acts sort of like a mission statement, plainly describing the story you're going to deliver.

Below that you'll see boxes lined up for each act. In the top row:

2.) This is the plot row, where you describe the organic three-act structure of the external story or main conflict. You can fill in these boxes by breaking the simple story concept into its three component parts:

- In Act 1 the goal is created.
- In Act 2 the goal is pursued.
- In Act 3 the pursuit of the goal is resolved – the goal is achieved or not.

In the middle (Act 2) box I like to state what the main conflict is (as an X vs. Y), as a reminder to build that conflict specifically as I continue developing the story.

3.) The next row down is the character transformation row. Each section of the screenplay needs to accomplish its function in the character arc or transformation:

- Act 1: Show us a protagonist who needs the transformation.

173

- Act 2: Show how the experience of this story causes the protagonist to learn the thematic lesson.
- Act 3: The protagonist demonstrates his transformation.

So in these boxes, describe how the three acts of character transformation work in your story.

And then connected to the character boxes are specific aspects of the character's transformation. Fill them in so you can make sure to include them as you develop the story further:

4.) At the beginning of the story, the character demonstrates a character flaw or misbehavior or other behavior strategy that's not serving them as well as they think. It's a survival strategy that is about to end its usefulness to the character. And it's usually the character's defining quality in the story.

5.) The thematic lesson is what the whole story builds toward. It's a realization or shift in thinking that changes the protagonist (hopefully for the better). It's the takeaway message, or point of the story.

6.) The transformed state is how the character behaves once they've embraced the thematic lesson and put it into practice. It's what's different about them. Proof the experience was transformative and had meaning.

7.) The CDQ is basically just turning the "someone wants something" of your story into a question. This is the question that's posed by your story, and what the audience is tracking in Act 2 (& 3).

Having it here in front of you reminds you that this is the open loop in the audience's mind. It's what they're waiting to have answered or satisfied. So the screenplay needs to stay pretty closely focused on what the protagonist is doing to answer the question, the progress and setbacks in relation to it, etc.

There's a space at the far right side to write down how the CDQ is answered, as well.

8.) And finally, a timeline of your screenplay with the major plot points marked in. Remember it's okay (great, in fact) to focus on 'what' needs to happen, rather than trying to figure out specifically 'how' it plays out on screen just yet.

Example story & structure worksheet: *Finding Dory*

For reference, here's an example of what an almost-completed worksheet might look like if you were working on a project called *Finding Dory*.

7. PUTTING IT ALL TOGETHER

You'll notice I've left the major plot points blank. I hope you'll take this opportunity to practice what you've learned by watching the movie and filling in the rest of the worksheet. (And you can always email me for the answer key, if you're curious.)

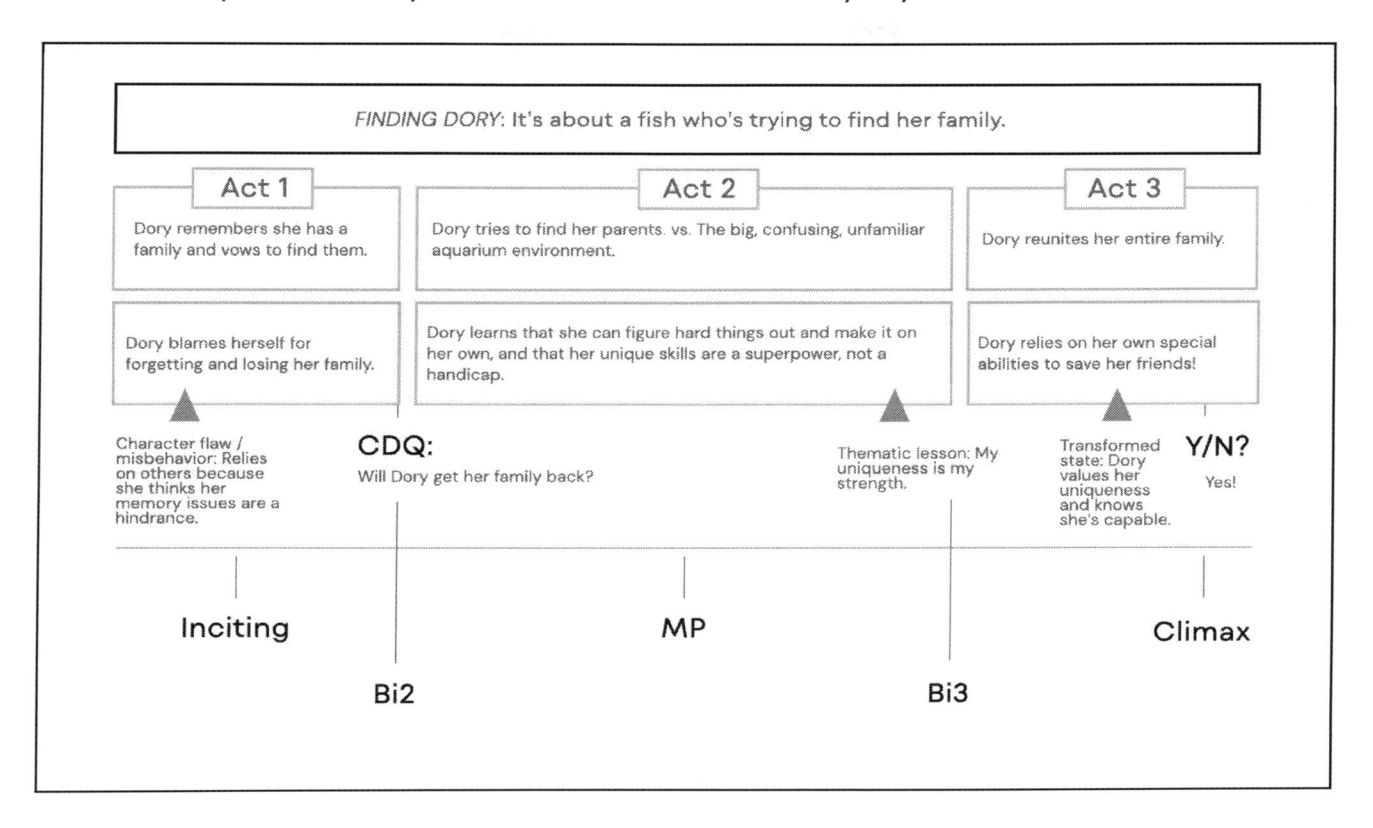

FINDING DORY: It's about a fish who's trying to find her family.

Act 1
Dory remembers she has a family and vows to find them.

Act 2
Dory tries to find her parents. vs. The big, confusing, unfamiliar aquarium environment.

Act 3
Dory reunites her entire family.

Dory blames herself for forgetting and losing her family.

Dory learns that she can figure hard things out and make it on her own, and that her unique skills are a superpower, not a handicap.

Dory relies on her own special abilities to save her friends!

Character flaw / misbehavior: Relies on others because she thinks her memory issues are a hindrance.

CDQ: Will Dory get her family back?

Thematic lesson: My uniqueness is my strength.

Transformed state: Dory values her uniqueness and knows she's capable.

Y/N? Yes!

Inciting | Bi2 | MP | Bi3 | Climax

175

THE SCREENPLAY OUTLINE WORKBOOK

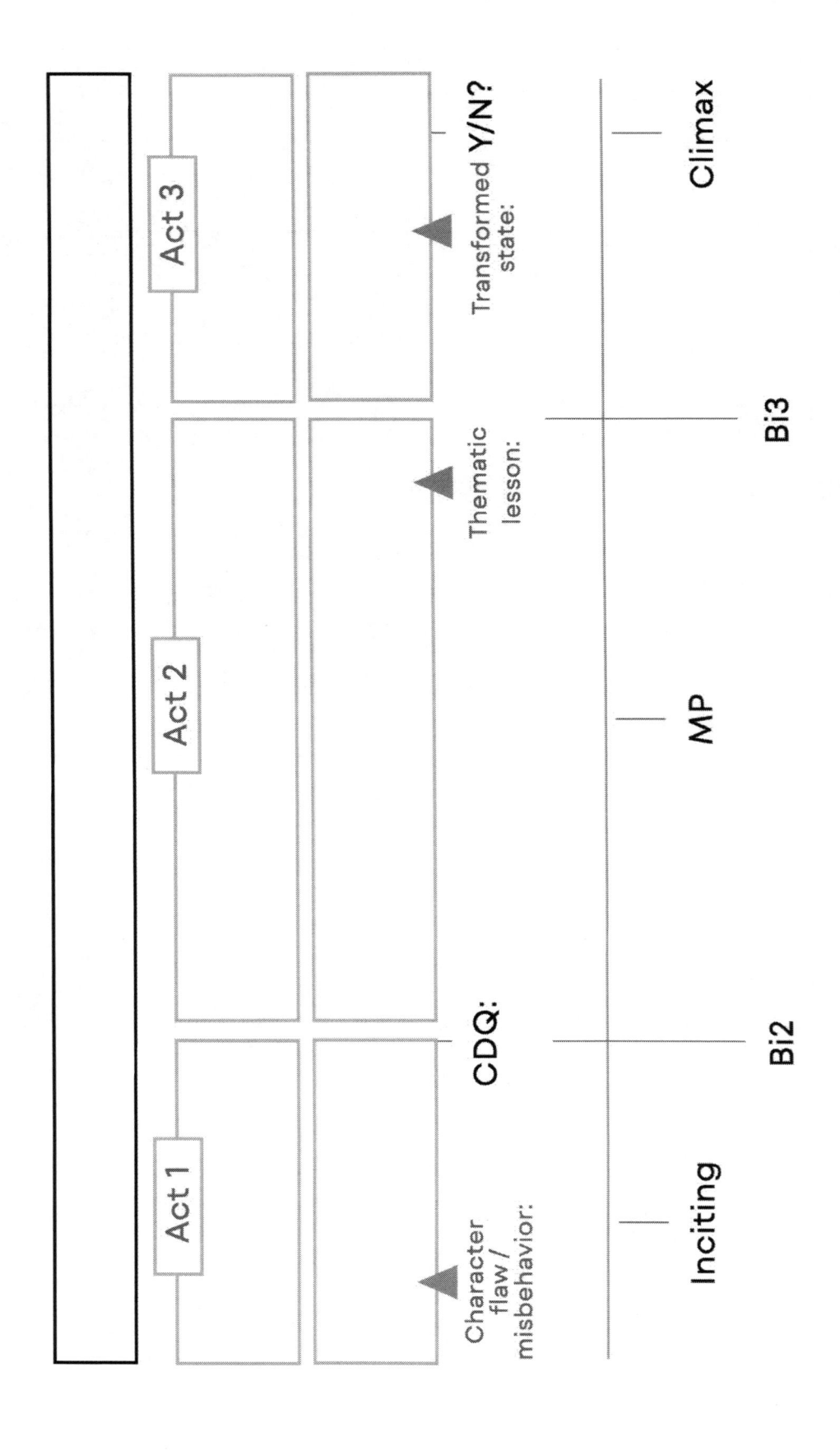

Act 1	Act 2	Act 3

Character flaw / misbehavior: ▸

CDQ:

Thematic lesson: ▸

Transformed state: ▸ Y/N?

Inciting —— Bi2 —— MP —— Bi3 —— Climax

176

7. PUTTING IT ALL TOGETHER

Notes

THE SCREENPLAY OUTLINE WORKBOOK

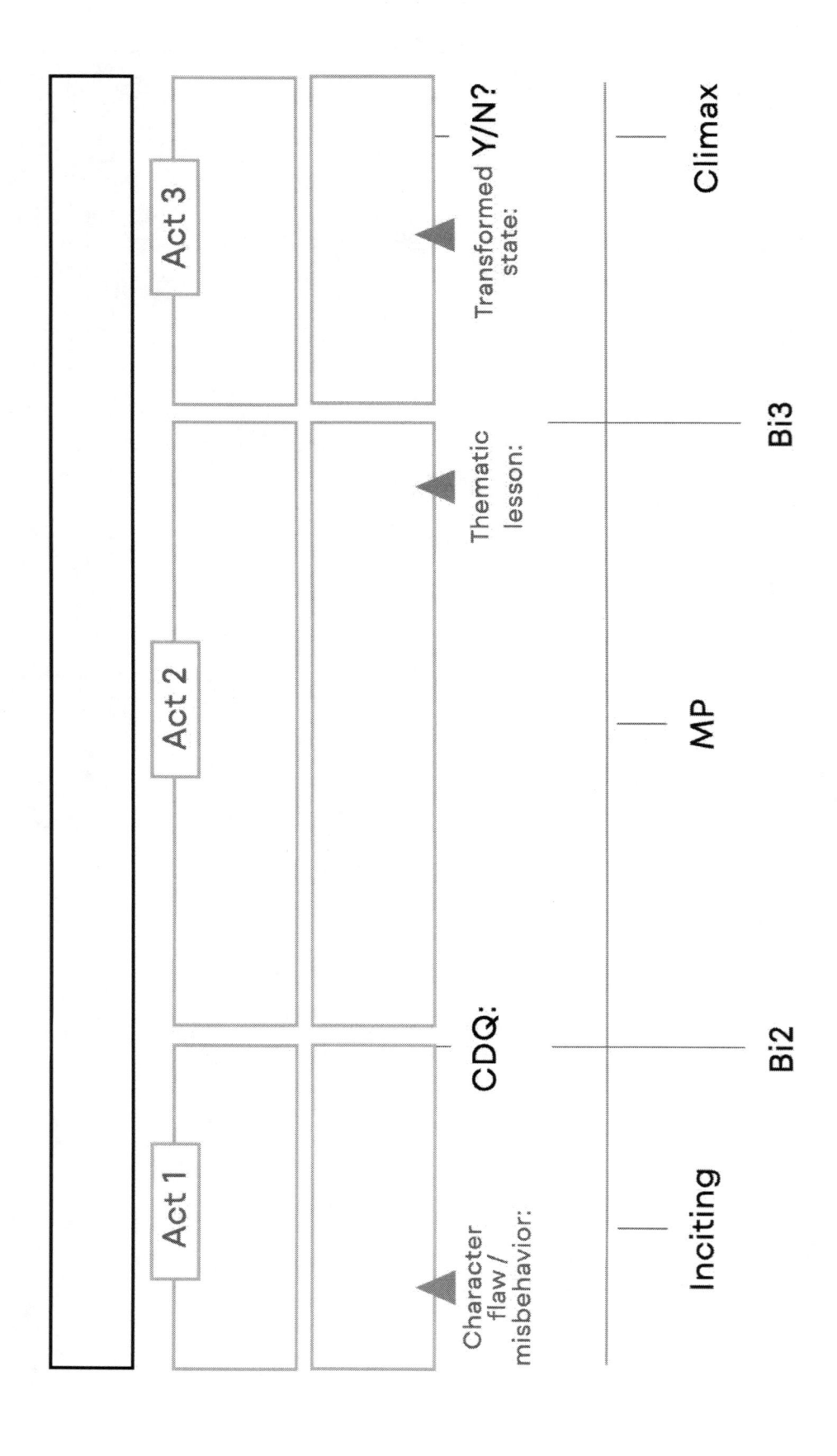

	Act 1	Act 2	Act 3
	Character flaw / misbehavior:	CDQ:	Thematic lesson:	Transformed state: Y/N?

Inciting — Bi2 — MP — Bi3 — Climax

178

7. PUTTING IT ALL TOGETHER

Notes

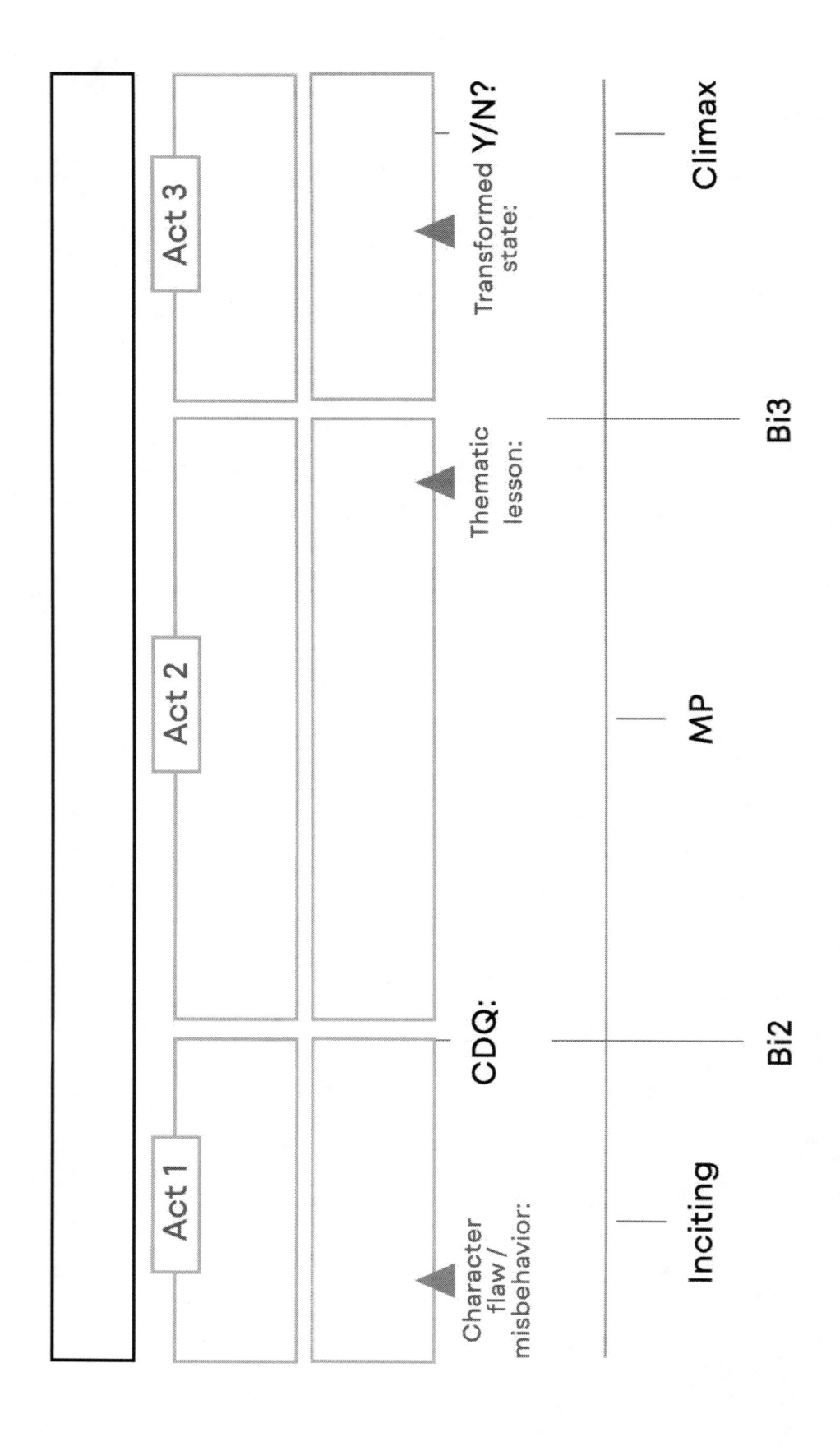

THE SCREENPLAY OUTLINE WORKBOOK

Act 1	Act 2	Act 3

Character flaw/misbehavior: ▲

CDQ:

Thematic lesson: ▲

Transformed Y/N? state: ▲

Inciting — Bi2 — MP — Bi3 — Climax

180

7. PUTTING IT ALL TOGETHER

Notes

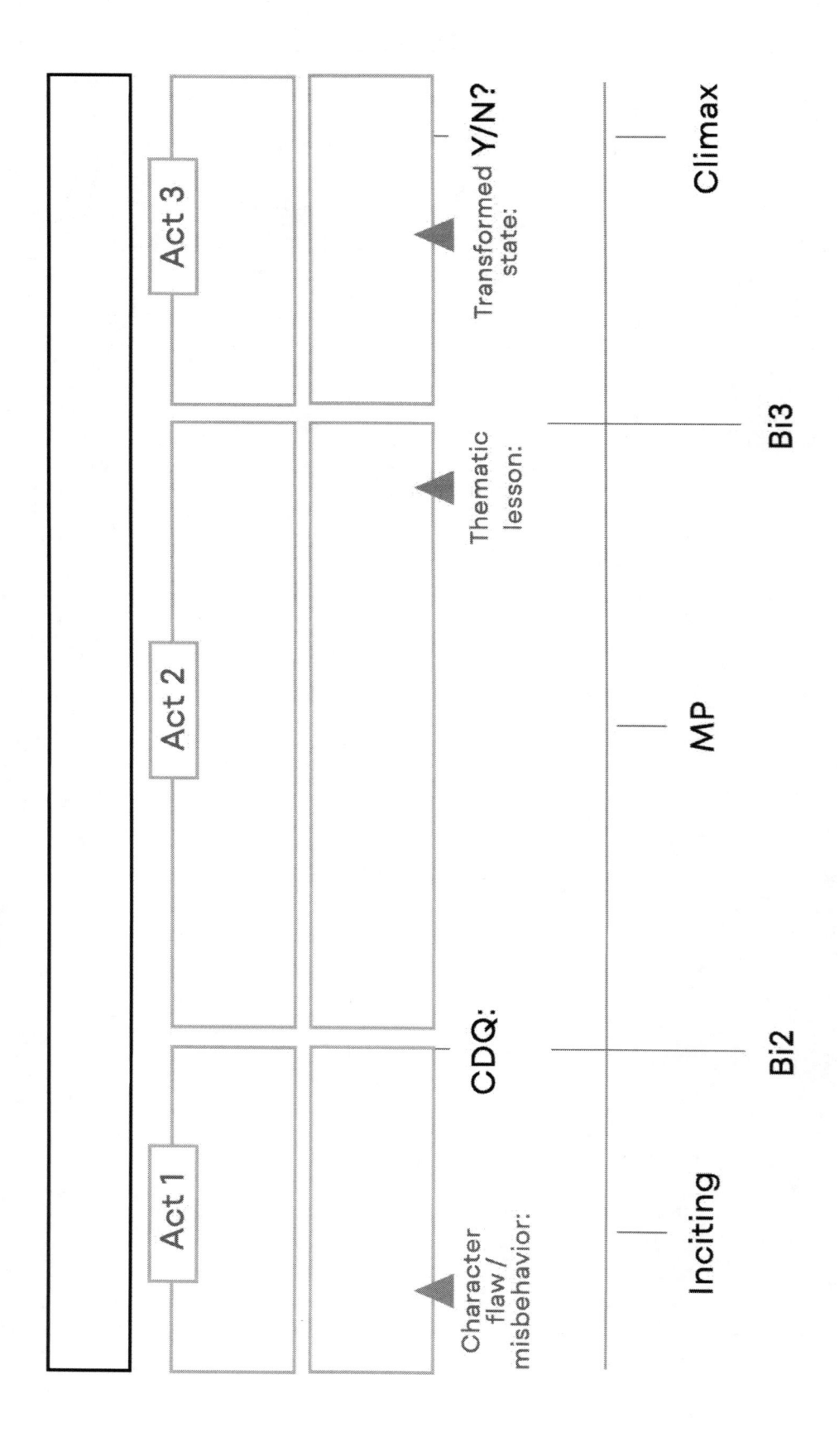

THE SCREENPLAY OUTLINE WORKBOOK

Act 1	Act 2	Act 3
Character flaw / misbehavior: ▶	CDQ: Thematic lesson: ▶	Transformed Y/N? state: ▶

Inciting — Bi2 — MP — Bi3 — Climax

182

7. PUTTING IT ALL TOGETHER

Notes

Your Screenplay Outline

The strategies I've laid out here can be used separately or together as you work out your story. Remember that this isn't a linear process. You might start with a simple story chart then move to sequences & springboards to break the story down further. When the story is figured out at that level, you might then find it makes sense to move to notecards on a board as you plan the story progression in more detail.

These are tools to keep in your toolkit, to use and experiment with, but there's really no magical key or single trick that will outline your screenplay for you. It all comes down to thinking through the story, adding, tweaking, finessing until the movie you see in your head is conveyed on the page.

By now, if you've done the exercises in this workbook, you've worked out your story from different angles and in some detail. You've assembled your entire story in one format or another. This part of the pre-writing process is about working out the specifics to a level you're comfortable with and that gives you the confidence to start writing.

And, as John August and Craig Mazin discussed, an outline is kind of what you decide it is. It's whatever style and format of document works best for *you*, because it's a map to guide you through writing your screenplay draft.

Your sequences & springboards? That could be considered an outline. Taking all of your notecards and typing them up into a list? Also an outline. The best outline is one that helps you write and finish your screenplay, and that may be different for every writer.

So your final step is to create your outline. The reveal here, though, is that your outline can be whatever you want it to be.

Screenplay Outline Example – *A Quiet Place*

This is the point, of course, where writers throw up their hands in frustration and say, *"Just show me what an outline looks like!"*

Which I get. For as much as I can say that it matters less what it looks like and more that it works for you, I also know how useful it can be to have a concrete example to guide you as you're feeling your way through the process of putting your own outline together. It gives you a target to aim for.

So the next three examples are documents I reverse-engineered from the movie *A Quiet Place*. These documents are not meant to represent the writers' actual creative work – I haven't seen inside their specific process. Instead, these are examples to show how a document might evolve as you develop an idea through this phase.

7. PUTTING IT ALL TOGETHER

Sequences & Springboards

Sequence 1: Post-apocalyptic world. A family scavenges in a looted grocery store. They're all concerned with not making noise.

Inciting Incident / SB 1: Youngest son makes noise, gets killed by creature.

Sequence 2: Over a year has passed, the family continues to survive in this world. They've adapted more. Learned more about the creatures. Mom's now pregnant. All still grieving loss of son/brother. Relationship between dad and daughter is strained.

Break into Act 2 / SB 2: We see the danger is still present and very real when kids accidentally make a noise and everyone reacts; the family's safety depends on everyone. Killed raccoon drives it home. (*Note: Story goal = Family's survival.*)

Sequence 3: The family prepares for the future. Dad's trying to make a hearing aid for daughter, but is also sheltering her. She thinks he blames her for brother's death.

Springboard 3: Dad won't let daughter come along with him and son to collect fish.
(*Note: Because of this event, the next sequence happens, i.e. daughter's frustrated and runs away, and son confronts dad about what's really going on emotionally.*)

Sequence 4: Dad and son navigate the world outside the farmstead. Dad learns he's sending wrong message to daughter. Meanwhile, daughter runs away.

Midpoint / SB 4: Mom goes into labor.
(*Note: Increases difficulty of them achieving their goal since she's about to GIVE BIRTH while trying not to make any noise. She's also about to be really vulnerable, which increases the difficulty of the family surviving intact and raises the stakes. Having a new family member raises the stakes as well.*)

Sequence 5: Mom tries to give birth without getting killed by a creature. Dad and son try to help and make it back to her.

Springboard 5: Dad finds mom safe with new baby.
(*Note: Because of this event, the next sequence happens -- dad's found mom and baby so he has to get them to safety. That means that son and daughter are on their own for a while. They've had good training, but son is scared so he's mostly hiding. Daughter knows what to do, though, and she finds her brother.*)

Sequence 6: Son and daughter make their way to each other and reunite. Mom and dad get to safety of basement bunker with baby.

Break into Act 3 / SB 6: Dad leaves to go find son & daughter. (*Note: This begins the new/final push to achieve the goal – family's survival.*)

Sequence 7: Son and daughter work together to survive and endure a creature attack. Reunite with dad just in time for another creature attack.

Springboard 7: Dad sacrifices himself (after telling daughter he loves her).

Sequence 8: Kids make it back to basement with mom and new baby. (Family is whole again, albeit a new configuration.) They manage to stay alive and figure out how to battle the creatures using hearing aid feedback.

Breaking down sequences into beat ideas

As a next step I'm simply taking each sequence description and brainstorming the individual story beats needed to accomplish what I've described.

Sequence 1: Post-apocalyptic world. A family scavenges in a looted grocery store. They're all concerned with not making noise.

- Introduce family – mom, dad, deaf older sister, middle brother, youngest brother.
- Show world – abandoned storefronts, no one else around.
- Top priority is being quiet.

Inciting Incident / SB 1: Youngest son makes noise, gets killed by creature.

Sequence 2: Over a year has passed, the family continues to survive in this world. They've adapted more. Learned more about the creatures. Mom's now pregnant. All still grieving loss of son/brother. Relationship between dad and daughter is strained.

- Life on farm. Adaptations for safety.
- Dad's research tells us details about creatures.
- Mom's pregnant.
- Strained relationship between dad and daughter because they're all living with grief and self-blame.
- Son and daughter help around the house.

Break into Act 2 / SB 2: We see the danger is still present and very real when kids accidentally make a noise and everyone reacts; the family's safety depends on everyone. Killed raccoon drives it home.

7. PUTTING IT ALL TOGETHER

Sequence 3: The family prepares for the future. Dad's trying to make a hearing aid for daughter, but is also sheltering her. She thinks he blames her for brother's death.

- ⋄ Dad tries to make hearing aid for daughter, daughter doesn't want it.
- ⋄ Mom's preparing to give birth and have a new baby join the family.
- ⋄ Brother is now terrified and doesn't want to leave the farm, but needs to in order to learn how to survive.

Springboard 3: Dad won't let daughter come along with him and son to collect fish.

Sequence 4: Dad and son navigate the world outside the farmstead. Dad learns he's sending wrong message to daughter. Meanwhile, daughter runs away.

- ⋄ Dad and son collect fish. Son is terrified, so dad explains the "rules" of noise.
- ⋄ Son tells dad daughter thinks he blames her.
- ⋄ Daughter runs away.
- ⋄ Mom does chores around the house.

Midpoint / SB 4: Mom goes into labor.

Sequence 5: Mom tries to give birth without getting killed by a creature. Dad and son try to help and make it back to her.

- ⋄ Mom has to let others know there's an emergency.
- ⋄ Mom's trying not to make noise while she's in labor, and creature stalks her in the house.
- ⋄ Dad and son see signal and carry out emergency plan.
- ⋄ Daughter sees the plan from afar.

Springboard 5: Dad finds mom safe with new baby.

Sequence 6: Son and daughter make their way to each other and reunite. Mom and dad get to safety of basement bunker with baby.

- ⋄ Son's alone and terrified. He hides.
- ⋄ Daughter finds son, they reunite.
- ⋄ Dad takes weakened mom and new baby to the bunker they've been preparing, while creatures stalk them.
- ⋄ Mom realizes kids are still out there somewhere.

Break into Act 3 / SB 6: Dad leaves to go find son & daughter.

Sequence 7: Son and daughter work together to survive and endure a creature attack. Reunite with dad just in time for another creature attack.

- Mom and new baby have to evade another creature that's gotten into the bunker.
- Son and daughter face a creature attack, end up hiding. Creature leaves after being affected by daughter's hearing aid.
- Dad finds the kids and reunites with them, but another creature's coming for them.

Springboard 7: Dad sacrifices himself (after telling daughter he loves her).

Sequence 8: Kids make it back to basement with mom and new baby. (Family is whole again, albeit a new configuration.) They manage to stay alive and figure out how to battle the creatures using hearing aid feedback.

- Kids make it back to basement to reunite with mom and baby.
- Daughter sees all of dad's work.
- While creature attacks, daughter figures out the hearing aid is helping them.
- Mom and daughter work together to kill the creature.

Expanding the beat list

Next I'd take that initial beats brainstorm and expand it to flesh out each sequence, adding some character detail, filling in relationships, even specific scene ideas – anything that comes to mind as I work through the story. Discovering more and more of what I will be writing into the screenplay.

Remember, this is creative work. We're just doing it in the pre-writing phase, rather than trying to figure all of this out while staring at a blank screenplay page. So the process will be experimental and messy, but hopefully fun.

And it's worth noting again that this is not my story, so these are not the actual documents written while the story was being developed. It's a mocked-up example to give you an idea of what the process might look like.

Sequence 1: Post-apocalyptic world. A family scavenges in a looted grocery store. They're all concerned with not making noise.

- Introduce family – mom, dad, deaf older sister, middle brother, youngest brother.
- Show world – abandoned storefronts, no one else around.
- Top priority is being quiet.

    - *An abandoned town, 'Missing' posters.*
    - *A family scavenges in a looted grocery store. We meet deaf older sister and youngest brother – he wants a rocket toy.*

7. PUTTING IT ALL TOGETHER

- o *Mom's getting meds for ill middle son.*
- o *Youngest son almost makes a noise – everyone reacts.*
- o *Dad/daughter relationship – solid.*
- o *Dad says youngest son can't have the rocket toy – "too loud" – but sister secretly gives it to him.*

Inciting Incident / SB 1: Youngest son makes noise, gets killed by creature.

- o *Walking home, youngest boy makes noise. Dad's too late. Creature grabs him.*

Sequence 2: Over a year has passed, the family continues to survive in this world. They've adapted more. Learned more about the creatures. Mom's now pregnant. All still grieving loss of son/brother. Relationship between dad and daughter is strained.

- ⋄ Life on farm. Adaptations for safety.
- ⋄ Dad's research tells us details about creatures.
- ⋄ Mom's pregnant.
- ⋄ Strained relationship between dad and daughter because they're all living with grief and self-blame.
- ⋄ Son and daughter help around the house.

- o *Day 472. The family is still surviving. Adapted to this life.*
- o *Dad studies and tries to make contact with other survivors.*
- o *Mom's now pregnant. Prepares baby's area; a box, oxygen tank/mask.*
- o *Alone, Dad grieves lost son.*
- o *Kids prep walls of bunker.*
- o *Dad lights fire atop grain silo.*
- o *Dinnertime. Daughter doesn't want to "call" dad for dinner, but mom makes her go.*
- o *They pray before eating. We see daughter pull hand away from dad's.*

Break into Act 2 / SB 2: We see the danger is still present and very real when kids accidentally make a noise and everyone reacts; the family's safety depends on everyone. Killed raccoon drives it home.

- o *After dinner, kids play Monopoly. Accidental noise/fire.*
- o *Tense waiting to see if the creatures will come. Noises on roof – just raccoons.*
- o *Elsewhere on the farm, we see the raccoon killed by the creature.*

Sequence 3: The family prepares for the future. Dad's trying to make a hearing aid for daughter, but is also sheltering her. She thinks he blames her for brother's death.
- ⋄ Dad tries to make hearing aid for daughter, daughter doesn't want it.
- ⋄ Mom's preparing to give birth and have a new baby in their join the family.

- Brother is now terrified and doesn't want to leave the farm, but needs to in order to learn how to survive.

    - Late into the night, Dad's busy in his workshop trying to make a hearing aid for daughter.
    - Mom and Dad have a tender moment, slow-dancing together – sharing music in their earbuds.
    - Day 473. Mom checks BP; due date is coming soon. Listens to baby's heartbeat.
    - Daughter tries to go into dad's workshop, he tells her to stay out (doesn't want her to see all his scary research). But shows her the new hearing aid he built. She doesn't want it. "It won't work." He gives it to her anyway.
    - Son's scared to go with dad to collect fish. Mom tells him he needs to learn these things, to be able to take care of himself, to take care of her when she's old.

Springboard 3: Dad won't let daughter come along with him and son to collect fish.

   - Daughter wants to go with dad to collect fish, but dad won't let her. "Just stay here. You'll be safe."

Sequence 4: Dad and son navigate the world outside the farmstead. Dad learns he's sending wrong message to daughter. Meanwhile, daughter runs away.

- Dad and son collect fish. Son is terrified, so dad explains the "rules" of noise.
- Son tells dad daughter thinks he blames her.
- Daughter runs away.
- Mom does chores around the house.

    - Upset and left behind, daughter tries new hearing aid. Doesn't work. She's frustrated. She packs her bag.
    - By the river, Dad explains "rules" of making noise to son, so he'll understand how to keep himself safe.
    - At home, mom's doing chores – snags potato bag on nail. Almost makes noise.
    - Later, she revisits dead son's room.
    - Son asks dad why he wouldn't let daughter come and reveals to dad that daughter thinks he blames her for son's death. "You should tell her you love her."
    - Daughter puts toy rocket on memorial.
    - Dad and son see dead woman; husband on the edge. He screams – alerts creatures. Son and dad have to run and hide as creature descends on old man.

Midpoint / SB 4: Mom goes into labor.

7. PUTTING IT ALL TOGETHER

  - *Mom goes into labor.*

Sequence 5: Mom tries to give birth without getting killed by a creature. Dad and son try to help and make it back to her.

- ◇ Mom has to let others know there's an emergency.
- ◇ Mom's trying not to make noise while she's in labor, and creature stalks her in the house.
- ◇ Dad and son see signal and carry out emergency plan.
- ◇ Daughter sees the plan from afar.

  - *Mom goes to basement. Steps on that darn nail and makes noise. She manages to flip the switch to alert others of emergency.*
  - *We see there's now a creature in the house. Mom endures contractions and tries to stay quiet. Sets timer.*
  - *Arriving back, Dad and son see red lights. They put into motion their plan – dad sends scared son to the "rockets", telling him mom needs his help.*
  - *Mom tries to stay quiet with creature stalking her nearby. The timer goes off, distracting the creature. She gets away.*
  - *Mom makes it to the bathtub in labor. The creature's still in the house, hunting her.*
  - *Son sets off fireworks.*
  - *Daughter sees them from the memorial and heads back. Dad gets his rifle.*

Springboard 5: Dad finds mom safe with new baby.

  - *Dad creeps through the house with his rifle at the ready. He sees the destruction. Fears the worst. Finds blood in bathroom. Breaks down in tears. Then – mom makes a noise in the shower stall, where she's slumped, spent. Mom and new baby are okay.*

Sequence 6: Son and daughter make their way to each other and reunite. Mom and dad get to safety of basement bunker with baby.

- ◇ Son's alone and terrified. He hides.
- ◇ Daughter finds son, they reunite.
- ◇ Dad takes weakened mom and new baby to the bunker they've been preparing, while creatures stalk them.
- ◇ Mom realizes kids are still out there somewhere.

  - *Out in the cornfield, son's alone. He panics at noises. Runs.*
  - *Dad carries mom and baby to the bunker. Baby starts crying and a creature starts stalking them.*

THE SCREENPLAY OUTLINE WORKBOOK

- *Dad hurries to put baby in a box with oxygen mask – something they'd prepped earlier.*
- *Daughter notices a light deep in the cornfield. She doesn't see a creature behind her. Before it can attack, it's struck by the sound of her hearing aid feedback. The creature can't take it and leaves.*
- *Mom wakes from dream of lost son. She realizes the other kids are gone. Dad tells her: "I'll find them." Mom reveals her feelings of guilt/regret over son's death.*
- *Daughter finds her brother. They hug, reunited.*

Break into Act 3 / SB 6: Dad leaves to go find son & daughter.

- *Dad goes out to find kids.*

Sequence 7: Son and daughter work together to survive and endure a creature attack. Reunite with dad just in time for another creature attack.

- Mom and new baby have to evade another creature that's gotten into the bunker.
- Son and daughter face a creature attack, end up hiding. Creature leaves after being affected by daughter's hearing aid.
- Dad finds the kids and reunites with them, but another creature's coming for them.

- *Daughter and son light the signal fire on grain silo. Daughter doesn't think dad's coming.*
- *Mom notices flooding in basement. Then sees a creature nearby. Mom gets the baby and hides behind "waterfall" where creature can't hear them as easily.*
- *Son falls into the grain silo. The noise alerts dad to their location, but the creature too.*
- *Struggling in the grain, the daughter saves brother, he saves her back.*
- *Creature arrives in the silo, but can't take the hearing aid feedback. It breaks out of the silo, leaving an out for the kids.*
- *Dad reaches silo. Reunites with kids. Mom watches her family on monitors.*
- *Dad hears a creature coming. Sends the kids to the safety of the truck. They watch as dad is hit by the creature. Son screams.*
- *Daughter turns off her hearing aid and the creature attacks the truck.*

Springboard 7: Dad sacrifices himself (after telling daughter he loves her).

- *Dad sacrifices himself (after telling daughter he loves her).*

Sequence 8: Kids make it back to basement with mom and new baby. (Family is whole

7. PUTTING IT ALL TOGETHER

again, albeit in a new configuration.) They manage to stay alive and figure out how to battle the creatures using hearing aid feedback.

- ⋄ Kids make it back to basement to reunite with mom and baby.
- ⋄ Daughter sees all of dad's work.
- ⋄ While creature attacks, daughter figures out the hearing aid is helping them.
- ⋄ Mom and daughter work together to kill the creature.

  - *Back at the farmhouse, Mom and kids reunite. But there are creatures coming.*
  - *Daughter finally gets to see dad's workspace. She sees all the effort he was making to give her a hearing aid.*
  - *A creature arrives in the basement. Daughter sees the monitor screens scramble and the creature can't take it the feedback. Daughter puts it together. She turns her hearing aid on again to make more feedback. The creature's knocked out.*
  - *The creature gets up. Mom shoots and kills it.*
  - *On the monitors they see more creatures are coming. Mom/daughter know they can now use the noise and the rifle to kill creatures.*

Beat/scene list screenplay outline

And here's the complete list, all in one place, in what most people think of as a typical outline format:

1. An abandoned town, 'Missing' posters.
2. A family scavenges in a looted grocery store. We meet deaf older sister and youngest brother – he wants a rocket toy. Mom's getting meds for ill middle son.
3. Youngest son almost makes a noise – everyone reacts.
4. Dad/daughter relationship is solid.
5. Dad says youngest son can't have the rocket toy – "too loud" – but sister secretly gives it to him.
6. Walking home, youngest boy makes noise. Dad's too late. Creature grabs him.
7. Day 472. The family is still surviving. Adapted to this life.
8. Dad studies and tries to make contact with other survivors.
9. Mom's now pregnant. Prepares baby's area; a box, oxygen tank/mask.
10. Alone, Dad grieves lost son.
11. Kids prep walls of bunker. Dad lights fire atop grain silo.
12. Dinnertime. Daughter doesn't want to "call" dad for dinner, mom makes her go.
13. They pray before eating. We see daughter pull hand away from dad's.
14. After dinner, kids play Monopoly. Accidental noise/fire.

15. Tense waiting to see if the creatures will come. Noises on roof – just raccoons.
16. Elsewhere on the farm, we see the raccoon killed by the creature.
17. Late into the night, Dad's busy in his workshop trying to make a hearing aid for daughter.
18. Mom and Dad have a tender moment, slow-dancing together – sharing music in their earbuds.
19. Day 473. Mom checks BP; due date is coming soon. Listens to baby's heartbeat.
20. Daughter tries to go into dad's workshop, he tells her to stay out (doesn't want her to see all his scary research). But shows her the new hearing aid he built. She doesn't want it. "It won't work." He gives it to her anyway.
21. Son's scared to go with dad to collect fish. Mom tells him he needs to learn these things, to be able to take care of himself, to take care of her when she's old.
22. Daughter wants to go with dad to collect fish, but dad won't let her. "Just stay here. You'll be safe."
23. Upset and left behind, daughter tries new hearing aid. Doesn't work. She's frustrated. She packs her bag.
24. By the river, Dad explains "rules" of making noise to son, so he'll understand how to keep himself safe.
25. At home, mom's doing chores – snags potato bag on nail. Almost makes noise.
26. Later, she revisits dead son's room.
27. Son asks dad why he wouldn't let daughter come and reveals to dad that daughter thinks he blames her for son's death. "You should tell her you love her."
28. Daughter puts toy rocket on memorial.
29. Dad and son see dead woman; husband on the edge. He screams – alerts creatures. Son and dad have to run and hide as creature descends on old man.
30. Mom goes into labor.
31. Mom goes to basement. Steps on that darn nail and makes noise. She manages to flip the switch to alert others of emergency.
32. We see there's now a creature in the house. Mom endures contractions and tries to stay quiet. Sets timer.
33. Arriving back, Dad and son see red lights. They put into motion their plan – dad sends scared son to the "rockets", telling him mom needs his help.
34. Mom tries to stay quiet with creature stalking her nearby. The timer goes off, distracting the creature. She gets away.
35. Mom makes it to the bathtub in labor. Creature's still in the house, hunting her.
36. Son sets off fireworks.
37. Daughter sees them from the memorial and heads back. Dad gets his rifle.
38. Dad creeps through the house with his rifle at the ready. He sees the de-

struction. Fears the worst. Finds blood in bathroom. Breaks down in tears. Then – mom makes a noise in the shower stall, where she's slumped, spent. Mom and new baby are okay.

39. Out in the cornfield, son's alone. He panics at noises. Runs.
40. Dad carries mom and baby to the bunker. Baby starts crying and a creature starts stalking them.
41. Dad hurries to put baby in a box with oxygen mask – something they'd prepped earlier.
42. Daughter notices a light deep in the cornfield. She doesn't see a creature behind her. Before it can attack, it's struck by the sound of her hearing aid feedback. The creature can't take it and leaves.
43. Mom wakes from dream of lost son. She realizes the other kids are gone. Dad tells her: "I'll find them." Mom reveals feelings of guilt/regret over son's death.
44. Daughter finds her brother. They hug, reunited.
45. Dad goes out to find kids.
46. Daughter and son light the signal fire on grain silo. Daughter doesn't think dad's coming.
47. Mom notices flooding in basement. Then sees a creature nearby. Mom gets the baby and hides behind "waterfall" where creature can't hear them as easily.
48. Son falls into the grain silo. The noise alerts dad to their location, but the creature too.
49. Struggling in the grain, the daughter saves brother, he saves her back.
50. Creature arrives in the silo, but can't take the hearing aid feedback. It breaks out of the silo, leaving an out for the kids.
51. Dad reaches silo. Reunites with kids. Mom watches her family on monitors.
52. Dad hears a creature coming. Sends the kids to the safety of the truck. They watch as dad is hit by the creature. Son screams.
53. Daughter turns off her hearing aid and the creature attacks the truck.
54. Dad sacrifices himself (after telling daughter he loves her).
55. Back at the farmhouse, Mom and kids reunite. But there are creatures coming.
56. Daughter finally gets to see dad's workspace. She sees all the effort he was making to give her a hearing aid.
57. A creature arrives in the basement. Daughter sees the monitor screens scramble and the creature can't take it the feedback. Daughter puts it together. She turns her hearing aid on again to make more feedback. The creature's knocked out.
58. The creature gets up. Mom shoots and kills it.
59. On the monitors they see more creatures are coming. Mom/daughter know they can now use the noise and the rifle to kill creatures.

Full scene-by-scene outline excerpt

For those writers who *really* like to think through as much as possible before writing screenplay pages, there's one more step you might consider: a full scene-by-scene outline.

This level of detail in an outline is usually more familiar to TV writers than to feature writers, but why let TV writers have all the fun? It's another tool you might find useful if you're a plan-first type of writer.

This step is a way to inch toward writing the screenplay. It allows you to continue to think through your story and screenplay in small, manageable increments. You can even format the full scene-by-scene document with your screenwriting software, so that the next step – writing the first draft of the screenplay – becomes a task of expanding this outline document rather than writing screenplay pages from scratch.

In the full scene-by-scene outline we'll take our previous document and begin to shape the individual scenes, describing what happens in each one. Some items on the list may already be scene-ready. Others may be story beats that we need to think through how to dramatize the information in a scene (or scenes).

Continuing with our *A Quiet Place* example documents, if we take our beat/scene list and isolate the first sequence (through the Inciting Incident):

1. An abandoned town, 'Missing' posters.
2. A family scavenges in a looted grocery store. We meet deaf older sister and youngest brother – he wants a rocket toy.
3. Mom's getting meds for ill middle son.
4. Youngest son almost makes a noise – everyone reacts.
5. Dad says he can't have the rocket toy – "too loud" – but sister secretly gives it to him.
6. Walking home, youngest boy makes noise. Dad's too late. Creature grabs him.

...and flesh those out into a scene-by-scene outline, it would look something like this:

7. PUTTING IT ALL TOGETHER

EXT. MAIN STREET — DAY

A once quaint, small town commercial area. Now abandoned, storefronts are all empty. 'Missing' posters overflow a community bulletin board.

INT. GROCERY STORE — SAME

Silence. Abandoned aisles. Empty shelves. Small, barefoot feet scamper past. YOUNG SON (5) plays hide and seek with SISTER (12). We'll soon notice she's deaf; the already-quiet world is completely silent to her.

Sister and Young Son entertain themselves, drawing pictures on the floor. They sign back and forth to communicate.

PHARMACY AISLE

MOM (30's) picks carefully through the remaining selection of prescription bottles. Near her feet, MIDDLE SON (8), suffering from a head cold, slumps miserably.

TOY AISLE

Young son tries to pull a rocket toy from a high shelf. He slips, dropping the toy. Just before it hits the ground, sister manages to get under it. Saved. She's more relieved than you'd expect — there's something very important about being quiet in this world.

CHECKOUT AREA

DAD (30's) shows Sister his haul and explains: something to help amplify the radio signal, a pair of pliers just for her. She says thank you; pleased at the small luxury.

Dad's suddenly on edge. We see what he's seeing: Young Son is holding the rocket toy. Dad quickly but carefully takes it and removes the batteries. They all sigh with relief. He tells Young Son he can't keep the toy, signing "too loud."

The rest of the family files out. Sister hands the toy back to her brother, winking conspiratorially. She doesn't see him grab the removed batteries before following.

```
EXT. WOODED PATH

The family walks single-file. The path has been layered with sand
to dampen their footsteps. They're quiet, but not frightened.

A sudden noise shatters the silence. It's the rocket toy. Dad
reacts, running for Young Son. But he's too late — a CREATURE
leaps from the woods and snatches the boy from sight.
```

If you complete this process for your entire story, you'll basically be halfway through writing your first draft. And having the end game in sight is great motivation to finish your screenplay.

When to stop outlining and start writing your screenplay

How to Vet Your Screenplay Outline Before Writing Pages

A 40-Point Checklist

How Do You Know When You're Done Outlining a Screenplay?

When to stop outlining and start writing your screenplay

You've done all the things — brain dumped, brainstormed, organized, and fleshed out the outline for your screenplay. But how do you know when the outlining is done?

The truth is – and you may be sick of hearing this by now – there's no one "right" way to do things at any given point in your screenwriting process, and that includes outlining the screenplay. As screenwriter John August has said:

> "Unlike screenplay formatting, there is no official standard. Generally, an outline provides a breakdown of how a story will play out. Outlines can take different forms based on many different factors including purpose, level of detail, method of creation, and writer preference. Some are incredibly detailed, listing every beat. Others give only very broad strokes."

Still... if you're new or new-ish to screenwriting, it can be daunting to move from outlining to writing the screenplay itself. How do you know if you're on the right track? Have you put what you need in the outline? Is your outline actually *done*? It can feel like leaping into the abyss with no indication that your parachute will open when you need it.

And to that I say two things:

1. You're not leaping into a literal abyss, so you don't have to worry quite so much. No writing is wasted. If what you write in the first draft doesn't work you can rewrite it. You won't die from bad writing, I swear.

2. To make sure you have really thought through and planned your story, you can vet your outline by asking many of the same questions we'd ask of a finished screenplay. There will always be surprises and discoveries and things that need adjusting as you write. But you can check your work before moving onto writing screenplay pages, to make sure the foundation is sound enough to build on and to see if there's anything glaring you've overlooked up to this point.

The 40-point checklist you'll see in the next section will help you with that vetting process. Again, you don't have to use this checklist. But if you want a tool to give yourself a boost of confidence before pushing forward, then this list of questions will help.

How to Vet Your Screenplay Outline Before Writing Pages

If you outline pretty fully, with the intention of using your outline as a blueprint for your screenplay, then it makes sense that the outline would have all of the major elements of the story represented.

That's the point of outlining a screenplay, right? To figure out the story – at whatever level of granularity you choose. To give yourself a map – again, however detailed you prefer — to follow when you get into pages.

So to see how strong the outline is, we should be able to ask some of the same questions we'd ask of a screenplay. We should be able to see if the major components we'll want to see show up in the screenplay are accounted for in the plan for the screenplay — the outline.

A 40-Point Checklist

With that in mind, here's a checklist you can use to vet your outline. It's not intended to be a must-have list. This is a guide to help you look at your own work with an analytical eye.

1. Can this story be reduced to a single sentence along the lines of "someone wants something badly and goes after it against strong opposition"?
2. Is it clear who the protagonist is? (The "somebody" from the one-liner above.)
3. If you have dual protagonists (two main characters), do they share a common goal? If not, would the story be better told via one main character?
4. Does the main character make the majority of the decisions that drive the plot?
5. What do we know about the main character from the scenes in Act 1?
6. Is the Act 1 impression contrasted in some way with what we see of the main character in Act 3?
7. What goes wrong, creating a new problem, desire, or opportunity that the protagonist must act on? (This is the Inciting Incident.)
8. What will happen if the protagonist fails to solve this problem, satisfy this desire, or exploit this opportunity successfully? (The story stakes.) How do we know this? (Where is it shown in the outline?)
9. Where do stakes increase?
10. Where are new stakes added?
11. Who / what is the main antagonistic force? What do they want? How do we see this?
12. Throughout the outline, do we see the antagonist getting in the way of the protagonist achieving their goal?
13. Does the antagonist have something at stake? How / where do we see this?
14. At the end of the first act, is it clear what the protagonist's story goal is?
15. Is this goal achieved in Act 3? If not, is that a deliberate choice?
16. Does the protagonist pursue their goal constantly and urgently? Can you see

this in the outline?
17. In Act 2, does the protagonist face obstacles that result naturally from circumstances you set up in Act 1?
18. Does the main conflict intensify?
19. Do obstacles get harder to overcome?
20. Are new obstacles introduced?
21. Does the midpoint increase opposition, raise the stakes, and/or turn the action in a significant way?
22. Is there a "low point" or a dramatic ramping up of intensity or stakes at the end of Act 2?
23. At the beginning of Act 3, does the protagonist have a new or revised plan for how to achieve his/her goal?
24. Does the protagonist confront the antagonist in the climax?
25. Does the climax decide whether or not the protagonist achieves his story goal?
26. Is the climax built squarely on actions, decisions, and events that took place earlier in the story?
27. For every conflict introduced, is there ultimately a satisfying resolution of some kind?
28. Does every scene have a clear purpose that moves the story forward in terms of the plot progression, character arc, or both?
29. Do scenes feel causally linked from one to the next?
30. Are there scenes that could be removed without affecting anything in the story?
31. Does the plot track from beginning to end without any holes or logic bumps?
32. Does the plot progression repeat itself at all? If so, is there a deliberate reason for this?
33. Are there any subplots?
34. Are subplots intrinsically related and relevant to the main throughline or do they connect to the big thematic idea?
35. Does each subplot have a throughline with a beginning, middle, and end?
36. Are subplots all resolved by the end of the movie?
37. Does every supporting character play a valuable role in challenging, stimulating, or aiding the protagonist along their journey and/or growth?
38. Are there any characters who aren't absolutely needed?
39. Is there anything interesting, fresh, or surprising in the outline? Is there anything we haven't seen before in another movie?
40. Does the tone feel consistent from beginning to end?

How Do You Know When You're Done Outlining a Screenplay?

Really, it's never done. Not while you're still writing the screenplay, that is. And "writing the screenplay" is ongoing. Through many drafts. Often right up until the movie's in the can.

So at some point, you just have to accept that the outline is good enough for right now, and then start writing the screenplay itself.

You can do this whenever feels right to you, and that will be different for every writer. You do not have to wait for permission. Whatever you don't have figured out now, will be figured out later.

A few final words

It's amazing how much you can do to ensure a solid screenplay before you ever get to writing the pages of the screenplay itself.

The aim of this workbook has always been to help you move forward and make real progress turning the movie in your head into a fully-developed story that you're ready to set down onto the screenplay page.

Once you've worked through the workbook, I hope you feel confident and excited to get to the computer and start writing. Already you have:

- Generated new story ideas
- Chosen a strong idea as the first step in writing a great screenplay
- Built a sturdy foundation for your screenplay by finding the essential elements of the story
- Discovered the organic three act structure and major plot points that create the framework for the story
- Designed compelling characters that all help push the protagonist along a meaningful character arc
- Tried one or more methods for mapping out your story and created a blueprint for writing a rock-solid draft of your screenplay!

And while I've tried to include everything you'll need to get from the spark of inspiration all the way to a complete outline, remember that outlining – just like writing the screenplay – is an iterative process. You'll probably find yourself revisiting sections and improving your work along the way.

As you're outlining, don't be afraid to throw out one choice and try something new. No writing is wasted and it's all part of the process. Sometimes (like our characters) we have to experiment with what we don't want before we can recognize what we *do* want.

And outlines are much shorter and easier to make adjustments to than whole screenplays! Which means you can pretty quickly try out different choices with minimal time investment. With that kind of freedom, there's no reason not to let your creativity go and see where it takes you.

If you'd like to learn more about writing a great screenplay – whether it's your first or your tenth! – you can find additional resources at writeandco.com

Now – go write that screenplay!

Naomi Beaty

Made in United States
Orlando, FL
18 January 2024